The MultipleMind Method

The 7-Step Process for Solving Problems and Generating Eureka Ideas

Steve W Roche

Founder of The Ideas Crowd

Published by Dragonwood
First Published 2012

To discover other titles by Steve W Roche
visit www.steveroche.com

ISBN: 978-0-9571826-1-5

Copyright © Steve W Roche, 2012

Design by Sparkwave – **www.sparkwave.co.uk**

For more information:
www.wizeeka.com
www.ideascrowd.com

This book is dedicated to my lovely wife, my gorgeous son and to the Ideas People everywhere who make the world a better place with their Eureka Ideas.

Table of Contents

Preface

For over 30 years I have been fascinated by new ideas and the people and companies who come up with them.

- Where do Eureka Ideas come from? Is it just luck?

- Is there something different about the way that inventive people think and innovative companies work?

- If so, is there a method that anyone can learn and use to become creative?

So to write this book I embarked on what became an enormous research project to find the answers to these questions. In the end it took the best part of 18 months and 1,400 hours of study.

- I read about the lives of the legendary and modern-day inventors, entrepreneurs and people from the world of arts and the creative industries.

- I delved into the history and workings of the great innovative companies.

- I looked for the timeless wisdom on the subject.

- I discovered the methods and techniques for creative thinking.

- I learned from the modern-day experts on the subject.

- I studied the latest scientific research on how the brain works.

The more I found out, the more captivated I became. I tested out the mindsets and techniques for myself and others.

In looking for a theory and a system, I had a Eureka moment of my own. It all came together. I identified the common traits and the essence of how Eureka Ideas are born and Ideas People work.

I have not discovered anything new, as such. However, what I have done with The MultipleMind Method is bring it all together into a philosophy and a set of techniques which anyone can use.

Eureka Ideas

According to myth, Archimedes was asked by his king to find out whether a crown was made of pure gold. The king thought that the goldsmith might have added silver. Archimedes knew he had to find a way of measuring the volume of the crown. He would have known what to do if it had been a standard shape.

Archimedes struggled to find the answer to the problem. That was until one day when he went to the public baths. The answer came to him in a flash. When the idea struck he leapt out of the bath and ran home naked shouting, "Eureka!"

His Eureka Idea came as he climbed into the bath. As he did so he noticed that water was displaced. Archimedes realised that the volume of water displaced was equal to the volume of the object placed into the water. This meant that he could measure the density of the crown and compare that to a bar of pure gold. In a flash he had found a way to work out the purity of gold by applying the principle of specific gravity.

What is a Eureka Idea?

A Eureka Idea is when the answer to a problem suddenly occurs to you seemingly out of nowhere. Eureka is a Greek word which means "I have found it".

The moment when a Eureka Idea hits you is also sometimes known as an insight or an epiphany.

A Eureka Idea feels different to when you have an ordinary idea. You feel triumphant and have a sense of achievement.

Examples of Eureka Ideas

Trace most brilliant ideas back to where they came from and you find that they originated from a Eureka moment.

One night in 1902, for example, a young American engineer called Willis Carrier was waiting for his train to arrive. He was watching as the fog rolled in across the platform when a Eureka Idea hit him in a sudden flash.

He realised that he could use the principle of fog to cool buildings. Carrier patented the idea and went into business. He turned his insight into the invention we know now as air conditioning. He made a fortune from his insight.

Jacob Davis ran a shop in Nevada making wagon covers and tents. One day in 1870 a customer came to him asking if he could make a cheap pair of trousers for her husband who was a gold miner. Her problem was that the pockets on his current trousers tore when he put the nuggets of gold he found into them. She begged him to make the trousers as strong as possible.

It was this comment that triggered Jacob's Eureka. His idea was to strengthen the pockets and button fly with the same copper rivets that he already used to attach straps to horse blankets. Right then, the idea for Levi's jeans with copper rivets was born.

Your very own Eureka software program

Your brain is no different to that of Archimedes, Willis Carrier or Jacob Davis. It has the same ability. It runs the same software.

Think about a computer that you own. Is there a useful bit of software on it that, for a while, you didn't know was pre-installed? Perhaps you found it because one day someone told you about it. Or maybe you discovered it by accident. Or possibly there's a handy software program that you used to use but had forgotten about and have recently rediscovered.

Well there's the equivalent of a software program that is pre-installed in your brain. Let's call it the *Ideation* software program. At the heart of every computer there is what is called the operating system. A computer is just a dumb box without it. At the heart of your brain's operating system is the *Ideation* software program.

You may have used *Ideation* a few times in the past, particularly when you were a very young child. You were almost certainly not told about it at school. If you were, you probably weren't told how to use it properly. You certainly wouldn't have been given an instruction manual.

What is really interesting about the *Ideation* software program inside your head is that it is like a computer software program that can connect to the Internet. A computer program that connects to the Internet is more powerful than one that doesn't. It can do more because it is not a standalone system. It is connected.

The *Ideation* software program inside your brain can connect with the brains of other people. As you will learn later, it does this in obvious and mysterious ways. It is hugely more powerful at what it does because of this.

Ideation

The word 'ideation' means the process of forming an idea. In other words, it means to conceive or imagine. How often do you hear people using the word ideation in everyday life? Did you have ideation lessons at school alongside core subjects like Maths, Science and English? Or have you ever attended a training course at work to learn about *Ideation*?

In fact until now, have you ever heard anyone actually use the word? But, arguably, ideation is the single most important thing that any of us should be doing at school or work.

What you're going to learn here is how to become an ideation expert. *The MultipleMind Method* is your instruction manual for your *Ideation* software program.

Think like a child again

You come alive again when you use your creative abilities. You become a kid again. Children are full of ideas. They are wonderfully enthusiastic and open to new things. They have fun and live with a spirit of adventure. They're imaginative and endlessly curious. It's such fun being around young children. They ask great questions. They take stuff in and they have wonderful ideas. They don't care what other people think and they are daft. These are some of the traits of highly creative people and the great Ideas People from history.

> *"Every child is an artist.*
> *The problem is how to remain*
> *an artist once he grows up."*
>
> Pablo Picasso

As we get older we start to lose our sense of fun, adventure and curiosity. Perhaps 'lose' is the wrong word, though. 'Neglect to use' might be a more accurate way of describing what happens.

Rediscover your passion for life

So many adults don't enjoy their lives. They hate their jobs and their home life suffers. It's not meant to be this way. We're not meant to live 'buttoned down' lives.

Think back to when you last had a really good or great idea. It may have been a really long time ago but if you think hard enough you will remember a Eureka moment. Do you remember what you were like?

Recall the sense of excitement that you felt. I bet you couldn't wait to share your idea with other people.

You have probably allowed your school, your workplace, the media and society as a whole to crush your innate creativity and to wipe out your spirit of adventure. Be courageous. Be a rebel.

Your brain is like a muscle. The more you use it to generate ideas, the better it will get at generating ideas. It gets better with practice, and not worse with age. The more you engage your brain, the more there will be to life.

Most people are a volcano of fantastic ideas when they first start work. But that eventually gets drummed out of them. Eventually they learn to do as others do. They do things 'the way they are done around here'. They end up mentally constipated and stagnated. Eventually they just give up. After all, what's the point?

Rekindle your spirit of adventure. Get back to when you believed that anything was possible. Believe that great and wonderful things could happen. If you do you will rediscover your passion for life.

The Ideas Age

We've been living through what has been called The Information Age for the last few decades. Other names that have been used for this period are The Computer Age and The Digital Age.

The Information Age got its name because we now have the ability to access and transfer information in a way that was never previously possible.

During this period we've seen the computerisation of mundane and routine tasks that used to provide jobs for people. The Internet has opened up the world. People are now being forced to compete with workers all over the planet for jobs. Businesses of all sizes now compete with companies from all over the globe.

Western countries have prospered during the last 30 to 35 years during The Information Age. As well as computerisation, another trend has been what the great writer and management consultant Peter Drucker called 'knowledge work'. Knowledge work is developing and using knowledge and then offering that as a service. Examples of knowledge workers include software developers, lawyers, consultants and accountants.

However, there's been a trend over the last few years whereby this type of work can be done in less time by information technology. Very often it can also be done cheaper and better in lower-cost countries that have a highly-skilled, English speaking population. With the high-speed communication systems we have today, if a business task is a step-by-step process, very often it can be easily done overseas.

So Information Age work has steadily been moving east, just as Industrial Age work like manufacturing has been doing for years. China has become the world's factory. It's now the turn of Information Age work such as software development, bookkeeping and other back office administrative tasks to be offshored.

A new era in the history of the world

Whether you've noticed it yet or not, we've entered a new period in business history. In the west we're saying goodbye to The Information Age and we're welcoming The Ideas Age.

What is this period going to be about? In short, it is a time when ideation skills will become increasingly important. No less a figure than Alan Greenspan, the former chairman of the Federal Reserve Board, said as much in a speech as far back as 1997: "The growth of the conceptual component of output has brought with it accelerating demands for workers who are equipped not simply with technical know-how, but with the ability to create, analyze, and transform information and to interact effectively with others."

The 'conceptual component' of jobs will become more important. It's where the value will be added. Creative people are going to become in high demand. Businesses of all sizes and in all industries will increasingly need new ideas and the people who come up with them. Society as a whole also needs new ideas and the people who come up with them like never before.

This is the Ideas Revolution. This new era is about creativity, innovation and design skills. These activities, because of their very nature, cannot so easily be outsourced.

The contributing editor of *Wired* magazine Daniel H. Pink calls this new period The Conceptual Age. He says that this phase in business history will be dominated by imaginative, right-brain thinkers as opposed to the logical, left-brained thinkers that have thrived in the industrial and information ages.

In his best-selling book *A Whole New Mind: Why Right-Brainers Will Rule The Future* he explains: "We've progressed from a society of farmers to a society of factory workers to a society of knowledge workers. And now we're progressing yet again – to a society of creators and empathizers, of pattern recognizers and meaning makers."

Aside from the world of business, the need for inventiveness is beyond question. There are social and economic challenges all around us crying out for creative solutions. The world is in crisis, and it's one of our own making.

> **"The last few decades have belonged to a certain kind of person with a certain kind of mind – computer programmers who could crank code, lawyers who could craft contracts, MBAs who could crunch numbers. But the keys to the kingdom are changing hands."** Daniel H. Pink

A new approach is needed

Old solutions won't work. As the great Albert Einstein said many years ago: "We can't solve problems by using the same kind of thinking we used when we created them."

Daniel H. Pink says that, in the last few decades, most of the thriving professionals were those who excelled in 'left-brain thinking'. This means people who perform tasks like information processing, analysis, logic, organization, numeracy and attention to detail.

But now information is getting easier to obtain. You used to need a degree to get hold of cutting-edge knowledge. Now much of that same knowledge is widely and cheaply available. So much of the information and knowledge processing that needs doing in the world of work can now be either automated or performed cheaply by highly-qualified professionals overseas.

So left-brain skills are still needed but there are other ways of getting that work done. So, as an individual, in order to do well in this new era you need to develop your right-brain thinking skills and to combine them with your left-brain thinking skills to become a 'whole-brain' thinker. In short, you need to become an Ideas Person.

Ideas People

"Ideas shape the course of history." John Maynard Keynes

Ideas People are capable of coming up with original and valuable ideas. Ideas People are whole-brain thinkers who combine the use of left and right-brain thinking skills. They also know the best way of tapping into the brains of other people.

An Ideas Person is someone who:

- follows a process;

- is extraordinarily curious;

- loves and cares about ideas;

- mixes and matches different ideas to come up with new combinations;

- is always looking for new connections between different ideas;

- shares their ideas with other people even if they're not sure about them;

- can appear illogical and contradictory; and

- is endlessly asking questions such as:

- "What if …?"
- "In what ways …?"
- "Supposing we …?"
- "Would it be possible to …?"
- "If we could …?"

An Ideas Person is also someone who is a divergent thinker. The majority of people think in a convergent way most of the time.

Convergent thinking is the opposite of divergent thinking. It generally means the ability to give the 'correct' answer to standard questions that do not require significant creativity. It is the kind of thinking that focuses on coming up with the single, well-established answer to a problem.

It is most effective in situations where an answer readily exists and simply needs to be either recalled or worked out through decision making skills. Convergent thinking leads to a single best answer. An answer is either right or wrong. Take maths as an example of a subject where convergent thinking is called for. It is about there being one single and right answer to a question.

Divergent thinking, on the other hand, is where there are many possible answers to a problem. It's not another word for creativity. But it is an essential ability of an Ideas Person. Divergent thinking is typically spontaneous and free-flowing and is encouraged by nonconformity, curiosity, a willingness to take risks, and persistence. Divergent thinking is often used in conjunction with convergent thinking.

Idea generation systems

Coming up with ideas may appear to be a haphazard activity. This is because ideas do not come to you when you're in 'work mode'. They pop into your head when you least expect them to.

There is an underlying process behind the generation of all ideas. You can condition your brain to produce ideas at will. All of us have more creative ability than we realise. Being able to generate ideas has nothing to do with IQ.

You can think like a genius. If you follow a method that works, that is. Study anyone who is good at coming up with ideas and you'll find that they work to a system. A system is a nothing more than a set way of doing something that guarantees results.

You have to be disciplined to work in a structured way. But that is no bad thing. Being disciplined enables you to get any job done.

Why do new ideas have such a bad name?

Historically, creative thinking has been maligned in favour of logical thinking and analysis. These left-brain ways of thinking have been seen as more important and better because of the way that our economy and the world of work have evolved over the last two centuries.

Some people associate creativity with wackiness and impractical suggestions. Idea generation is not about being different for the sake of being different. Ideas must have value. But to come up with a really good idea you invariably have to work your way through some really bad ideas as well.

Creativity is like entering the unknown. It feels risky. But the truth is that these days it's riskier to be uncreative.

The greatest Ideas Person of all time

Thomas Edison was the greatest inventor in history. He owned 1,093 patents by the time he died.

It's staggering what we all owe to the inventiveness of Edison. His invention of the incandescent electric light bulb in 1879 significantly changed the way that people were able to live. Suddenly living could extend into the evening.

He put together what he knew about electricity with what he knew about gas lights and invented an entire system for providing power to communities.

His first invention came in 1868 when he created a Vote Recorder. He was a hugely productive inventor. Other notable inventions of his were:

- a printing telegraph in 1869;
- a stock ticker in 1869;
- an automatic telegraph in 1872;
- an electric pen in 1876;
- a phonograph in 1877;
- an electric motor in 1881; and
- a storage battery in 1900.

> **"None of my inventions came by accident. I see a worthwhile need to be met and I make trial after trial until it comes."** Thomas Edison

Edison was born in Ohio in 1847. He attended school for just three months. When he was 12 he began selling newspapers on the Grand Trunk Railway. He devoted his spare time to experimenting with printing presses and with electrical and mechanical contraptions.

In 1862 when he was just 15 years of age he published his own weekly newspaper which he called *The Grand Trunk Herald*. He moved to Boston to work and spent his spare time carrying out research.

Edison made $40,000 from selling telegraphic appliances and used the money to set up his own research laboratory in 1876. In 1887 Edison moved his laboratory from Menlo Park in New Jersey to West Orange, New Jersey.

Edison's system for invention

His most important invention was not a product or business idea, though. His greatest achievement was that he created a system for invention. He loved the process of invention as much as he loved the results. He funded and placed huge importance on his company's research and development efforts.

The following is a list of the ways in which Edison worked. This is his system of invention.

Hard work and high standards

Edison believed that good ideas come to you if you work hard and if you're strict with yourself. It is easy to be mediocre. He believed that people should be intolerant towards mediocrity.

Fail your way to success

Edison believed that the more times that you fail at something, the sooner you will succeed. Failure is nothing more than a hard lesson that needs to be learned. It directs you back to where you need to go.

This is something that Thomas Edison believed to the core of his being. Every time that he failed at something he made a note of what he'd done and readjusted the next time. He simply saw every failure as an experiment. He regarded failure as his friend. But he was obsessed. He would not quit until he got the answer he was looking for.

A life well-lived means that you will fail most of the time. You will fail 80% of the time. But that's OK as long as you learn the lessons.

"Nothing is more dangerous than an idea when it is the only one you have." Émile Chartier

Push yourself

Thomas Edison knew that to get better quality ideas you need to produce a large quantity of ideas. The best way is to set yourself targets. Set yourself ideas quotas. As General George S. Patton famously once said: "Pressure makes diamonds."

Creative people often procrastinate. So you can counteract that by putting pressure on yourself.

Genius is about thinking differently. Most people don't realise the importance of coming up with lots of ideas in order to get a good one. Remember this formula:

Prodigious = Genius.

If you produce a large quantity of ideas, many will be bad ones. The more ideas that you come up with, the more likely it is that you will generate original and valuable ones. The unoriginal and non-valuable ideas that you generate are the stepping stones towards the good ideas.

You will find that your best ideas will come in the latter stages of your idea generation process. One of the problems is that people give up too soon when they try to come up with ideas. The first few ideas are always the obvious ones. You've got to keep pushing.

The twilight state

Thomas Edison knew about a state of mind that he called the twilight state. It is where you can tap into the creative genius of the subconscious mind. It is a state of mind in between sleep and being fully awake.

Give 'em what they want

One of Thomas Edison's mottos was 'invent what the world wants'. He was constantly asking himself the question, "What are people crying out for?"

Do not work in the dark to create commercial and profitable ideas. Most people, it seems, invent products and business ideas before they've looked properly at the industry. As a result, they end up coming up with naïve ideas that have very little commercial value.

Identify your customer first. Then create and make them what they want. In other words, understand your prey.

Edison understood that you must provide something of value. It's the customer that determines whether you provided something of value to them or not. You must meet a customer need or want with your idea.

Bear in mind, though, that customers don't always know what they want in advance. They know what their problems and desires are, though. This is where you come in. You can come up with ideas and solutions if you know what their problems and desires are. They'll be able to tell you if what you have created is what they want. So it's all about knowing your customer.

Sleep on it

Thomas Edison used to take power naps. He found that he performed at his best when he slept twice a day. Once at night and once for a few hours during the day.

The mule rule

Thomas Edison never gave up. He believed in the Mule Rule. A mule keeps plugging away until it gets to its destination.

Big ideas can take time. Sometimes it helps to break them down into smaller chunks. Never, ever quit, though. You'll get to your destination in the end.

Just doodle it

Thomas Edison kept notes about everything. You should do the same. Also keep a journal or a diary so that you can record your life as it unfolds.

Sometimes it helps just to write things down that are on your mind. Great ideas often come in this way. It's called doodling and you let your mind run free. Do not edit what you write. Let your mind spin all over the place. Genius finds relationships between the most diverse of things.

Here's the process for doodling.

1. Give yourself a time limit.

2. Relax and write easily.

3. Write quickly and without stopping. Your mind thinks fast. If you're not sure what to say then just write down anything that comes to mind – literally. Write the same phrase over and over again if you need to. Just keep your pen moving on the page.

4. You don't have to write words. You can also draw.

Be bold

Edison knew that fortune favours the brave. Be bold. Many people fail because they are 'commitment phobics'. There is power in commitment.

> ## "Whatever you can do, or dream you can, begin it. Boldness has genius, power and magic in it!"
>
> Johann Wolfgang von Goethe

Play around

Edison was intensely curious and was fun to be around. The lesson here for you is to redevelop the level of curiosity and the sense of fun you had as a child.

There is scientific evidence which proves that your mind works better when you feel good. Always have fun. It doesn't matter if a deadline is approaching – mess around!

There is a part of the brain called the amygdala that triggers fear. It shuts down creativity when it kicks in. But when we're happy and having fun, guess what? The amygdala isn't doing its thing.

Work should be fun. This doesn't mean you should always be laughing. But it does mean that you will work best when you are passionately involved and love what you're doing.

You cannot have a big idea and make money unless you're having fun. This is because fun is how you generate and sustain the energy you need.

There are similarities between creativity and humour. The basis for most comedy is that your thoughts are first taken along a familiar and logical path. You are then taken off down an unexpected and illogical path, and this is the punch line.

Creativity has the same basis. Creative thinkers tend to be funny and humourous. They're good at connecting things which are not normally connected.

> **"These days, the problem isn't how to innovate; it's how to get society to adopt the good ideas that already exist."**
>
> Douglas Engelbart

Sell your ideas

One of Thomas Edison's greatest skills was being able to bring his ideas to the attention of people that mattered such as investors and the press. He was a showman. He was flamboyant and carried out stunts.

You must do whatever you can to communicate the power and desirability of your ideas. If you can't sell it, no one else will be able to. Don't be disheartened, however, if your ideas are initially rejected. This is quite normal. It takes time and effort to overcome the status quo.

Edison was also charismatic and hugely optimistic. He was able to make his staff believe in his dreams. He was also able to get his investors to feel the same way.

- He sought knowledge and answers relentlessly.

- He was rigorous and thorough.

- He was objective.

- He was a collaborator. He always believed that two heads were better than one.

- He knew that you need to be definite and have clear aims.

Edison understood human nature. He rewarded his staff but in ways that were not always financial. Many of his staff were not well paid but they wanted to work for him for the privilege of working with the great man.

The MultipleMind Method

The world needs Eureka Ideas. And it needs Ideas People to come up with them. But how? You're about to discover a method that you or anyone else can learn. When you follow the step-by-step process you will become an incredibly powerful Ideas Person able to come up with a Eureka Idea for any problem or situation.

Let's be clear from the start. Exciting, original and valuable ideas don't happen as a result of ordinary thinking. Ordinary thinking results in ordinary ideas.

The MultipleMind Method is an extraordinary form of thinking. The word extraordinary means "beyond what is usual, ordinary, regular, or established". *The MultipleMind Method* results in extraordinary ideas. It creates Eureka Ideas.

This is a system that you can use to come up with any kind of idea, be it large or small. When you use this method you reawaken and reinvigorate the powerful but dormant creative abilities inside you.

The MultipleMind Method works in a very particular way. You get every part of your brain working on the task. In other words, you use both your conscious and subconscious mind. You think in a 'whole brain' way using both the left and right hemispheres of your brain.

Our own minds – although way more powerful than we realise – are limited in that we each have a set number of experiences and thoughts to draw on. For this reason, the method also taps into the minds of other people.

As you will learn later, Eureka Ideas actually originate from what is called superconscious thinking. All the steps in *The MultipleMind Method* play a part in activating the superconscious mind.

The MultipleMind Method draws together:

- timeless wisdom;

- inventive thinking principles;

- the attitudes and techniques used by history's great entrepreneurs, thinkers, artists and inventors; and

- the latest cutting-edge scientific evidence on how the creative part of the brain works.

The name for the method comes from the fact that you use:

- the multiple thinking styles of your own mind;

- a multiple number of other people's minds; and

- the superconscious mind, which is sometimes also called the 'third mind'.

Colourful Thinking is the term used for the aspect of the method where you use your own mind in multiple ways. Crowd Creativity is the term used for the facet of the process where you tap into the minds of a diverse range of other people.

Colourful Thinking

You probably spend most of your day thinking in a frenetic, fast-paced and superficial way. Perhaps this kind of high-intensity and speedy 'beta wave' thinking has become habitual and is a way of life for you now. I call this DayTime Thinking.

Beta wave thinking has its place. For example, when it comes to analysis and action-planning. But if you spend too much time thinking in this way, you will feel tired and stressed.

Effective creativity comes from adding other thinking styles into the mix. It's like thinking in colour instead of in black and white, which is why I call this approach Colourful Thinking.

Other colours of thinking are as follows.

- The deep thinking which occurs when brain wave frequencies slow down and intensify. This happens when you sleep. We call this NightTime Thinking and it can be used to generate ideas and solve problems.

- The insights and inspirational thoughts which come from theta wave thinking, which we call DayBreak Thinking.

- The reflective and intuitive thoughts which come from alpha wave thinking, which we call DayDream Thinking.

> **"I not only use all the brains that I have, but all that I can borrow."**
>
> Woodrow Wilson, 28th president of the USA

Crowd Creativity

People have the ability to be extraordinarily inventive working on their own. However, each of us only has a limited amount of knowledge, skills and experiences to draw on for inspiration.

Science shows that two or more heads are better than one. If, that is, the 'multiple minds' work together in a particular way. You can't just assemble a group of people and as a result expect a high level of creativity. Anyone who has ever been to a business meeting knows this to be true only too well! Hidden agendas and antagonisms can immediately derail creativity.

There is a scientific basis to group creativity. We know from studies that certain conditions need to be in place for a group of people to be highly creative. Crowd Creativity is the set of attitudes and aptitudes for connecting and coordinating brainpower that will enable any group to collaborate effectively and generate a constant flow of original and valuable ideas.

Superconscious Thinking

The Superconscious Mind has been known about for thousands of years. But it's only in the last hundred years or so that we have begun to understand it fully. Sigmund Freud founded the discipline of psychoanalysis in the late 19th and early 20th centuries. He wrote about there being three minds which he called the ego, the id and the super ego.

- He defined the ego as the part of the mind which deals with the external world. It analyses, decides and takes action. In other words, this is the conscious mind.

- He said that the id is the part of the brain which stores memories, previous thoughts, knowledge and feelings. It works automatically and takes care of functions such ensuring your physical body operates without you having to think consciously about it. This is your subconscious mind.

- Freud called the super ego the third dimension of thought and he said it worked in the way described here in this book.

What can it be used for?

You can use *The MultipleMind Method* to create any kind of idea you like, be it for business or otherwise. When it comes to business, you can use it to:

- come up with an idea for a new business;
- improve any aspect of an existing business;
- create new products, services, or processes;
- improve old products, services, or processes; or
- find answers to complex business problems.

You can also use the method to improve a social or economic situation or to fix a problem in your local community. You can use it in your home life also.

The MultipleMind Process

You're now going to discover the seven step system for generating Eureka Ideas. Each step builds on the previous one. The sequence is an important part of process. This is because there is a time and a place for each type of thinking. For example:

- critical thinking is not suitable at the idea generation stage as it suffocates creative thoughts; and

- critical thinking is required after ideas have been generated in order to assess them properly.

The initial steps lay the groundwork for the later ones. There is:

- precise thinking at the start:

- turbo-charged inventive thinking during the middle of the process; and

- pragmatic thinking at the end so that ideas are turned into reality.

Points to bear in mind

- Clarity is power. Too often creativity efforts fail because the objectives are vague. The brain thrives when there is precision. For this reason a lot of time is devoted to defining the creative challenge.

- The brain responds well to deadlines and a sense of urgency so it's a good idea sometimes to set a time limit. Big ideas can take time to emerge, however. It's almost as if these Eureka moments bide their time until the effort has been put in.

- The Eureka Idea may hit you at any stage in the process. Record all the ideas that occur to you, though, as they may be useful in the future. It'll probably be at the end when you get your flash of insight, but be prepared at any point.

Step 1
Foundation

Many people mistakenly believe that they are no good at coming up with good ideas. The fact is that we all have enormous untapped reserves of creativity that we routinely fail to use. There is a huge amount of evidence that we are all creative.

Your own inventive thinking ability is there right now within you waiting to be used. It might be buried quite deep. Maybe it was repressed when you were younger. But it is there nonetheless. That is without question. You must have no doubt in your mind about your ability to come up with a Eureka Idea.

It is, of course, true that some people are naturally creative. The number is about one in seven people, it seems. But creativity and idea generation is a skill that can be learned by anyone.

Change your old habits and beliefs

Belief is so important. If you think of yourself as an Ideas Person then, with practice, you will become one. Your creative ability grows with practice.

Many of our beliefs are long-held conclusions that we came to based on our experiences when we were younger. All of our beliefs make sense at the time we form them. We find evidence to support them. But things move on. Do your beliefs make sense all these years on?

You must believe in your ability to do this. The ability is inside you. It just needs to be tapped. With the right outlook, you can tap your creativity and be successful with your ideas.

The process for generating ideas can be tough. Sometimes you can feel like you're not getting anywhere. You need to feel certain that you can generate great ideas. You're in trouble if you are uncertain and doubt that you can do it. You will still be able to come up with new ideas but they won't be a Eureka Ideas.

Inside your head right now is an extraordinarily powerful software program. But like a software program installed on a computer, you need to open it up if it's going to work. Believing that you can be good at generating ideas is the equivalent of opening a software program.

Also, the more times you use your ability to generate ideas, the better you will become. Practice is so important. Thinking is hard work, which is one of the reasons so many people avoid it.

Your ideas are very different when you feel that you are a creative person to the ideas that you come up with if you do not feel yourself to be creative. This is a very important point.

You must believe that there is something inside you that makes you equal to the rest of the world in terms of talent and ability in this area. Do not put yourself down.

Here are some exercises that you can do which will enable you to believe in your creative abilities.

Out with the old, in with the new

Before you can take on the new mindset, you need to ditch your old one. Take a blank piece of paper and draw a line down the middle. Write 'Out with the old' as the heading for the first column and write 'In with the new' as the heading for the second column.

Give yourself 30 minutes to work quietly on this task.

Write down all the negative things that come to mind when you think about your ability to come up with and do something about new ideas.

Things that you might write down could include:

- *"My ideas are never very original."*

- *"Someone has probably thought of my idea already."*

- *"My idea is too crazy to be taken seriously."*

Reflect on and examine these thoughts. When did you form these beliefs? What was the basis for them back then?

In the second column, for each of the beliefs come up with a positive statement that will become your replacement belief. Think about evidence from your past that can support that belief.

For example, as a counterpoint to "My idea is too crazy to be taken seriously" you could write down "Most of the world's greatest inventions were at first considered crazy."

> **"All truth passes through three stages. First, it is ridiculed. Second, it is violently opposed. Third, it is accepted as being self-evident."**
>
> Arthur Schopenhauer

Success breeds success

You do well when you feel good about yourself. Achieving success and thinking about success give your brain a rush of a feel-good chemicals including one called dopamine. Success feeds on success because dopamine makes your brain perform better.

So you will do better if you remember your past successes and don't dwell on your failures. Learn from your failures but do not keep thinking about them.

Look at Thomas Edison, for example. He didn't care how many times he had failed at something in the past. In fact, he didn't think of his failed attempts as failures. Small successes are stepping stones to greater ones.

> **"An inventor fails 999 times, and if he succeeds once, he's in. He treats his failures simply as practice shots."**
>
> Charles Kettering

This exercise is all about recognizing and remembering your successes, plus your good qualities and characteristics. It is also about forgetting your failures, but learning from them.

- Take a blank piece of paper. Give yourself 20 minutes for this task.

- Write down all the things that you like about yourself. Also write down all the achievements that you've had it in your life, both large and small. Keep writing for the whole time.

You will begin to experience more success if you make a habit of remembering your successes and good qualities and paying less attention to your failures.

> **"A man becomes what he thinks about, most of the time."**
>
> Ralph Waldo Emerson

Picture yourself as an Ideas Person

Did you know that we all act, feel and perform in line with our definition of who we are? So what is your current self-image? Whatever it is, you'll find that you think and behave in accordance with it. When you begin to think of yourself as something different, you will act, feel and perform differently.

So your task now is to create and reinforce a new self-image of yourself as an Ideas Person by using a couple of powerful techniques.

Picturing

Imagine what things will be like when you are living as a successful Ideas Person. Paint a picture of that in your mind in exquisite detail. Make this vision a multi-sensory experience. Involve all your senses as best you can. So see the sights, hear the sounds, feel the feelings, and so on.

Your subconscious mind doesn't know the difference between what is real and what is imagined. So if you picture yourself as having already achieved your desire, your mind will get to work on making it a reality.

Imprinting

The more often you can remember and picture your new self-image as an Ideas Person, the more likely it is to become a reality. The challenge is that we get so caught up in daily life that we forget about important issues. Imprinting is a way of burning that image into your mind so that it is with you all the time.

A way to do this is to find occasions when you will be reminded to picture your new self-image in your mind. Choose a short walk that you take on a frequent basis. For example, your journey to the local shops or the train station. Select landmarks on that journey. Make them your triggers for picturing your new self-image. When you actually pass these landmarks you'll remember to think about your new self-image in your mind.

7 Habits of Highly Effective Ideas People

The following behaviours will set you on your way towards becoming an Ideas Person. By taking on these new habits, you will encourage your brain to become more creative.

Take an Ideas Workout every day

The idea generating capacity of your brain is like a muscle. It gets stronger the more often and the harder you work it. Taking an Ideas Workout each day will make your brain better at generating ideas.

Here's what you do each and every day.

- Pick a regular timeslot.

- Give yourself the challenge of coming up with a set number of ideas each time.

- Shut yourself off from any distractions.

- Select a problem, a challenge or a goal that you need an answer to. You could work on the same problem, challenge or goal each day until you get the answer you need. Or you could vary what you work on each day.

- Allocate 15 minutes a day and set yourself a target of coming up with a minimum of 20 ideas in that period.

- Write down all the ideas that come to mind. Even include the ideas that may seem ridiculous or far-fetched.

What matters is that you do your Ideas Workout each day and that you keep going with it until you come up with your ideas quota.

What you're doing is forcing your brain to come up with ideas. You're telling it that you're serious about finding answers. It will respond. It'll probably come up with more ideas than the quota you set.

This is about giving your brain a creativity workout every day. You wouldn't go to the gym and lift weights once and expect to be a changed person, would you?

Thomas Edison believed in this approach. He set himself the target of coming up with:

- one major invention every six months; and

- one minor invention every 10 days.

Edison believed that he wouldn't have achieved very much if he hadn't set himself targets.

Start a Brain Box

Ideas are triggered by stimuli. The more you can expose yourself to new stimuli, the better you will become at generating valuable and original ideas.

So get yourself a big plastic storage box and label it 'My Brain Box'. As you come across new and interesting objects, press cuttings, magazine articles, photos, advertisements, etc put them in your Brain Box. Also print off and store interesting stuff you find on the Internet.

Every so often when you need an idea, pick out three random items from your Brain Box. See if looking at them triggers any new ideas.

Use an Ideas Catcher

> **"Every composer knows the anguish and despair occasioned by forgetting ideas which one has no time to write down."**
>
> Hector Berlioz

Most of the time good ideas will come to you when you least expect them to and when it's most inconvenient. So you need a way of catching ideas there and then.

If you don't, they will be gone. This is because we are only able to store five to nine pieces of information for about 12 seconds in our short-term memory. After 12 seconds we are very poor at recalling what was in our head. After 20 seconds the information will be gone completely.

The only two ways that you'll be able to recall the information is to either:

- keep repeating it to yourself; or
- write it down or capture it in some other way.

When you capture an idea in this way it acts as a signal to your brain that the information is important. It will then be stored in your long-term memory in a way that will enable you to recall it easily.

When you do this, your brain is relieved that you took notice of its idea. This will encourage it to provide you with more ideas in the future.

You need some kind of Ideas Catcher and you need to take it with you wherever you go.

Go for either:

- a good, old-fashioned notebook and pen;

- a digital voice recorder; or

- a smartphone or a tablet computer app.

My own personal favourite method is a smartphone app called Evernote (www.evernote.com). One its beauties is that it allows you to make written notes, take photos and record audio notes. And this can be done via its smartphone app and website.

Review the ideas you capture on a regular basis. You might see a connection between an idea and a present situation or problem.

Change your routines

We all need some level of routine in our lives. But you limit your ability to be creative if you're too regimented.

Are you one of those people who is a slave to their routines? Do you always do things the same way? Must everything be its place?

Creativity thrives on new input and experiences. It is the raw material that your brain uses.

Make a list of things that you do habitually. For one whole month try doing things differently. For example take different routes to work or eat foods that you've never had before. Your brain will thank you for it.

Learn to pay close attention

How well do you notice what is going on around you? There is a part of the brain called the Reticular Activating System (RAS). Its job is to notice what you notice.

It will notice what you program it to notice. If you program it to notice the bad points in other people, it will. If you ask it to look out for good opportunities, it will do exactly as you ask.

By learning to pay better attention you can look at mundane things in a new way. You can spot miraculous opportunities. Pay better attention to what's happening around you in everyday life and you'll be amazed at what you might spot. An idea can be found anywhere.

Exercise

- Find a detailed photograph or picture.

- Find somewhere where you can sit comfortably and be relaxed.

- Set a timer for 10 minutes.

- Look at the photograph or picture continuously without moving a muscle until the timer goes off.

- Stay focused. Do not allow your mind to wander. Only pay attention to the image in front of you.

- After the timer goes off, look away and recall the experience.

- Review the experience visually and not just in words.

You will be amazed at what you now begin to notice in everyday life. Do this exercise often to fine-tune your ability to notice things.

Be patient

Big ideas can take time to come to you. In any idea generating exercise the first few ideas you come up with will probably be unoriginal and obvious ones. You may then get a series of original but small ideas. But these 'small sparks' are often the building blocks for the 'big idea'.

Do not think that's it and give up. Keep going. One of the marks of a genius is that they're persistent.

Most people won't sit down and focus their thinking on a problem or challenge without interruption for as little as 15 minutes. Most people are not willing to do that, let alone go on the long haul looking for a big idea that may take weeks or months to happen.

"People think of the inventor as a screwball, but no one ever asks the inventor what he thinks of other people" Charles Kettering

Be crazy and have fun

You won't come up with great ideas unless you're prepared to think differently every so often. Most people spend their time conforming.

We are taught to only think and talk in a way which makes sense. We are taught to be logical. So introducing something completely random and unconnected to the current topic of conversation or problem we're working on is regarded as mad and nonsensical. But when we do, we open up the possibility of fabulous new ideas popping into our heads.

Fill your head with different stuff. Read magazines and visit websites for topics that you have no interest in. Talk to people you'd normally avoid at parties. Read poetry. Listen to kids.

Reality is not relevant. Most breakthrough ideas went counter to conventional thinking at the time. Don't look in your rear-view mirror. Look to the future.

> **" Almost all really new ideas have a certain aspect of foolishness when they are first produced. "**
>
> Alfred North Whitehead, English Mathematician and Philosopher

Don't worry what other people think. You must continue to think in terms of new possibilities. It's time to stop self-censoring yourself and holding your brain back.

Fun is fundamental. Examine the word fundamental. It means 'a central or primary rule or principle on which something is based'. Fun is a fundamental part of the process required to be inventive.

Did you know that the average child laughs 110 times a day? The average adult in their mid-40's laughs just 11 times a day.

Just to repeat: fun is a fundamental part of this whole process. A study was done a few years ago which found that people come up with three to five times more ideas when they're laughing.

> **Results? Why, man, I have gotten lots of results! If I find 10,000 ways something won't work, I haven't failed. I am not discouraged, because every wrong attempt discarded is often a step forward.** Thomas Edison

Don't be afraid to fail

You already have what you need. It was there when you were a small child. Back then, you used to dream and imagine freely. Your head was full of ideas. Children are happy to try and fail. They keep going.

Most adults are different. They're afraid to try and fail. They tend to stick to what they know they're good at.

But to get to an idea that has value you normally have to come up with a number of ideas that don't work. But ideas that don't work are not mistakes. They are good. They get you one step closer to the great idea.

Look after your new ideas. They may look ugly at first but nurture them so that they grow and flourish. Save them for later, if need be. You never know when they'll be useful to you.

Brain food

Did you know that certain foods have a big impact on your creativity? Numerous studies support the belief that eating the right kind of stuff can increase your brain powers.

Your brain uses:

- carbohydrates for fuel;

- omega 3 fatty acids as the building blocks for its neurotransmitters (these are the chemicals in the brain which transfer signals from one cell to another); and

- antioxidants help preserve its powers in the long term.

The fuel

Your brain gets its energy from carbohydrates. The best type is complex carbohydrates. They are sometimes referred to as starch or starchy foods. They break down slower, so steadily supply energy for many hours. Some examples are:
- bananas
- barley
- beans
- brown rice
- chickpeas
- lentils
- nuts
- oats
- parsnips

- potatoes
- root vegetables
- sweet corn
- wholegrain cereals
- wholemeal breads
- wholemeal cereals
- wholemeal flour
- wholemeal pasta
- yams

The other type is simple carbohydrates. An example is white bread, which burns fast and only gives you a short-term energy boost. Examples are:

- biscuits, pastries and cakes
- pizza
- sugary breakfast cereals
- white bread
- white flour
- white pasta
- white rice

Simple carbohydrates are also known as sugars. Natural sugars are found in fruit and vegetables.

You need to try and avoid all fast-acting carbohydrates such as sugars. Only eat them when you need a quick shot of energy. If you eat sugars all the time you will not be able to get a boost from them when you really need one. Think of yourself as a sports car. If you use high-performance fuel all the time, you'll quickly wear out your engine.

The building blocks

Ideas and information flow from brain cell to brain cell. Think of your brain as having a network of roads that run from cell to cell. Your brain builds these roads using oils.

The best type of oil is omega 3 fatty acids. If you don't eat enough foods that contain this type of oil then your brain is forced to build its roads with other types of oils. These other oils aren't as good for carrying information and ideas between your brain cells. So the processing power of your brain will be slowed down.

Omega 3 is present in a few foods but the best source is oily fish and nuts. It is good for the rest of your body as well.

Protection

You need to protect your brain from what are known as free radicals because they damage the tissues. You do that with anti-oxidants. The most well-known are vitamins C, E and beta carotene. You get vitamin C and beta carotene from fruits. Vitamin E is present in nuts.

Supplements

A natural substance that our body produces called creatine improves brain performance. You can normally buy it in health food shops. Don't use it indefinitely, though.

Stimulants

There are foods which can stimulate your brain by:

- speeding it up; or

- making it more creative by freeing your right brain from your left brain.

Don't overdo these stimulants though. If you do, you can affect your health and your long term creative output.

Speed boosters

Caffeine is an often-used stimulant these days. It is present in coffee, tea and cola.

Bear in mind, though, that it won't work if you drink it regularly. You should keep your body clear of caffeine until the time when you want to speed your brain up. If you drink it within about four hours of going to bed you won't sleep very well. It will disrupt your sleep patterns and you will wake up tired.

Other speed boosters are:

- sugars;
- taurine (which is found in eggs, dairy products, fish and red meat);
- gingko biloba; and
- gotu kola.

You should be able to buy gingko biloba and gotu kola from most health food shops.

These stimulants work by temporarily speeding up your metabolism.

Creativity boosters

The left hemisphere of your brain is the rational part of your mind. In many ways, it keeps your right brain in check. It keeps you rational but it can limit your ability to connect your thoughts and come up with new ideas.

You can partially block out your left brain with alcohol. Don't take too much, though. You need just the right amount to calm you down. You will become sleepy and will be unable to concentrate if you have too much.

If you eat a good diet then your normal state of mind will be calm and naturally creative.

These things also boost your creative powers.

- Sleep for 7 to 8 hours a night.

- Sport improves your brain power as it sets off feel-good chemicals.

- Listen to music as doing so relaxes your mind.

- Make friends as friendships increase your brain power.

- Scents and smells can stimulate your creativity.

Step 2 Clarification

"Clarity is power." Anthony Robbins

Coming up with ideas is not a haphazard activity. You need to direct your thinking. The Clarification step involves giving your brain very specific guidance on the Eureka Idea you want it to come up with.

The aim of this stage of the process is to write an Ideation Task (IT) Statement which precisely describes the Eureka Idea that you need. This is not easy to do sometimes but is worth the effort involved.

> *" A problem well stated is a problem half-solved."* Charles Kettering

In the same way that a river needs banks for the water that flows through it to reach its intended destination, your thinking needs to be given boundaries in order for your brain to give you the idea you want. No wind is the right wind for the captain of a ship if he doesn't know the port he should be headed towards. Your brain is like a heat-seeking missile. But it needs clear, specific goals. Vagueness doesn't work.

This sounds so logical, doesn't it? But it's amazing how rarely people do this. You will waste a lot of time if you try to come up with new ideas without a definite and measurable goal.

Types of ideas

Part of the clarification process involves understanding the nature of the idea you are seeking. Ideas fall into a few categories.

- Ideas which improve something that already exists.
  - We'll call these *improvement ideas*. Nothing is ever perfect. There is always some aspect of anything that can be made better. With improvement ideas, you need to be precise about what needs to be improved and have a way of measuring. Otherwise how will you know what you come up with is better? In what ways do you want it to be better? For example, is it cost, speed, quality, less complex, more satisfying, less waste, and so on?
- Ideas which create something brand new.
  - This is where you start from scratch. New inventions and the work done by creative professionals such as designers, writers, and architects fit into this category. We'll call these *creation ideas*.

- Ideas which solve a problem.

  - We'll call these *how-to ideas.*

- Ideas which enable you to overcome obstacles, make it happen and achieve a goal.

  - We'll call these *fruition ideas.*

How far down the road are you with your idea?

Not sure what kind of an idea you want yet?

Are you looking for a problem to solve? In other words, are you problem seeking? If so, think about what bugs you.

There are problems all around us. We just need to pay attention. If a problem irritates you then you can bet your bottom dollar that it irritates other people as well. Fix it and they'll pay you for the solution. Don't stay irritated. Find the answer.

Think back to when you've had good ideas in the past. The chances are that, to begin with, something had really annoyed you. It might have been bad service from a company or a poorly designed product. Out of that came your idea for how to do it better.

Look at Nature. I'm sure you'll agree that one of the most beautiful objects in the world is a pearl. A pearl grows as a result of an oyster being irritated if a foreign object gets between its mantle and its shell. The oyster covers up the irritant with layers of nacre to protect itself. This process eventually forms a pearl. Something beautiful is created as a result of an irritation.

You can use your frustrations as the basis for generating new ideas.

Create your own Bug List

- List all the things that annoy you. It could be a company, a product, a service, a situation or whatever. Also think about irritants that other people have told you about.

- Write down specifically what bugs you. Be as precise as you can about it.

- Go through your bug list. Pick out the ones that most interest you.

- Work on coming up with ideas that would resolve the problems using *The MultipleMind Method*.

Already aware of the problem you want to solve with an idea?

Thomas Edison was in this situation when he was trying to invent the incandescent electric light bulb. He already knew what he wanted his idea to do. He wanted to invent a lighting product. He just hadn't figured out how to do it. He eventually did of course, after more than 10,000 attempts.

So do you have the idea for what you want to create but don't yet know how to do it? If your challenge is an engineering one such as the one faced by Thomas Edison then when you get to step 4 in this process you might want to use a problem solving approach called TRIZ. You'll find full details at Appendix 1.

The Ideation Task (IT) Statement

You need to define the idea you are looking for in words. You must, must write it down. Doing so is the cue for your creativity to get to work.

Writing things down is when a thought becomes real for your brain. It's like giving your brain its marching orders or sending it an email. Writing it down is where the pipedream ends and the action begins. It gets your brain into production mode.

You'll recall that earlier I mentioned a part of your brain called the Reticular Activating System (RAS). It is the area responsible for regulating arousal. This means it reacts to stimuli. It controls what you notice and the things that catch the attention of your five senses. Your RAS gets to work when you set it up with a precise definition of what you are seeking. It will draw you to information, people and other resources that will help you to achieve your aim.

Creating your Ideation Task Statement

The more time you spend at this point in the process, the closer you will get to the idea you need. The less time you take, the more chance there is that you will get not-so-good ideas.

There are three sections to an Ideation Task Statement and they are:

- the problem;
- the purpose; and
- the question.

Start out by describing the problem that currently exists. Next, you need to set out the reasons why you want a Eureka Idea. This is because you never want to lose sight of the bigger picture as you set out seeking an idea. Describe the benefits you will get from the new idea.

So let's say you run a local restaurant and your business has been hit badly by the arrival of a new competitor. Your Ideation Task

Statement might start out as follows:

The Problem – The new Indian restaurant has taken all our best customers away.

The Purpose – We want to have a flourishing and a financially secure business once again.

The next part of the Ideation Task Statement is the specific and definite question that the Eureka Idea will provide the answer to. How you frame that question is very important. The question you ask shapes the answer you get.

Think about the problem from many angles. You need to question your assumptions about the problem you are going to solve. Remember the old saying: "Assume makes an 'ass' out of 'u' and 'me'."

Let's take another example. Say your local area is, in your opinion, being ruined by kids drawing unsightly graffiti all over public property.

You need to think carefully about how you frame your question and you should examine your assumptions. If you assume that the problem can be solved by spending more money you might phrase the Ideation Task Statement question as follows:

- In what ways can we lobby the local government to spend more money cleaning away the graffiti more frequently?

If the question is phrased in this way you are limiting the possible range of answers. You have *assumed* that the answer relates to money. It may, but it may not. Ask yourself whether that question –

with its built-in assumption – will yield a Eureka Idea that will resolve the root cause of the problem.

For example, we know that children and young adults become involved in graffiti vandalism for a number of reasons. They include gang association, peer recognition, lack of artistic and recreational alternatives, the element of danger, and a lack of appropriate parental supervision and discipline.

So, a better question might be:

- In what ways could we keep our local area free of unsightly graffiti in a way which enables the needs of children and young adults to be met as well?

This is a bigger challenge but one thing to bear in mind is that people tend to think of more innovative answers when they're given a bigger challenge to work on.

You arrive at a good Ideation Task Statement question by thinking about things from all angles. The broader the question is, the more likely you are to come up with ideas that take advantage of all the opportunities. The best type of question is one which reflects all aspects of the problem. An excellent way to phrase the question is to include the words "In what ways …?"

- So the wording for an improvement idea question could be: "In what ways could we improve …?"
- The wording for a creation idea question could be: "In what new ways could we …?"
- The wording for a how-to question could be: "In what ways could we solve the problem of …?"

So if we go back to our restaurant example, the Ideation Task Statement question could be:

- In what ways could we improve our marketing so as to bring our ex-customers back and to attract brand new customers?

The final Ideation Task Statement would then become as follows.

- *The Problem – The new Indian restaurant has taken all our best customers away.*

- *The Purpose – We want to have a flourishing and a financially secure business once again.*

- *The Question – In what ways could we improve our marketing so as to bring our ex-customers back and to attract brand new customers?*

With this crystal clear Ideation Task Statement, your brain now has got something definite to work with. It knows what the problem is, the benefit of solving it and precisely what kind of Eureka Idea is needed.

If sub-problems emerge as you work through the process, as they probably will, deal with those issues as well. In the restaurant example a question for a sub-problem could be:

- In what ways could we improve our window display so that more passers-by come into our restaurant?

It is worth experimenting with the wording. Slight changes can make a big difference. For example, try changing one word for a synonym. Or try adding new words.

For example, notice how this small word change affects the whole energy of the question:

- *In what ways could we improve our window display so that more passers-by are enticed to come into our restaurant?*

The question comes alive just by adding the word 'enticed'. This one change means that ideas will be sparked in your head that you would not otherwise have come up with.

Also, when you move to the next steps and start coming up with ideas, remember that you need to keep pushing for ideas. Quality will come from quantity. Keep asking "how else?" and you'll be amazed at how many other ideas will emerge.

Sometimes it can be difficult being precise about the idea you want to generate right from the start. So sometimes it's necessary to come up with a general question first of all, move onto step 3 and to then come back to this step to come up with a precise question.

Step 3
Saturation

"Genius is 1% inspiration, 99% perspiration" Thomas Edison

The creative process which produces Eureka Ideas appears mysterious. Eureka Ideas do normally look like bolts out of the blue as they strike you in a flash. But they're not bolts out of the blue at all.

There is a precise process that leads up to every Eureka Idea. They normally only emerge after a great deal of hard work. And it's at this stage of the process where most of the hard work is done.

"Opportunity is missed by most people because it is dressed in overalls and looks like work."

Thomas Edison

Pablo Picasso's art looks like the work of a once-in-a-generation genius. But when you examine his life you find that the young Picasso spent his early years painstakingly drawing parts of the human body.

His creative genius was also not evident in the early part of his career. But he continued to spend countless hours practicing and working at his craft. It was from trying and failing that he was able to develop his expertise.

His amazing creations were the result of him saturating his mind in his work. When his talent fully blossomed he unleashed a tidal wave of amazing work. But he'd put the work in beforehand that enabled this to happen.

Step 3 is the full concentration stage. There are three aspects to this phase.

Immersion
- This involves fully researching and gathering together relevant material on the subject that the Eureka Idea you are seeking relates to.

Inspiration
- This part of the process involves stimulating your brain with unrelated, random and diverse material.

Input
- This means talking about the problem with outside people but doing so in a very specific and deliberate way.

This is the stage of the process where you can expect ideas to start to come to you. Record all of them in whatever way you can – in writing, on a Dictaphone or on a smartphone app.

Immersion

Find out all you can about the area in which you are looking for ideas. There are many ways that you can carry out your research.

- Dig out all the information you already have stored on your computer or in books that you own.

- Visit the library.

- Carry out Internet searches on Google and the other major search engines such as Bing and Yahoo.

- Google Books lets you search and read excerpts from millions of books.

- Google Scholar allows you to search peer-reviewed articles, books, reports, theses, preprints, abstracts, technical reports, and conference papers.

- Visit dedicated research websites such as:

    - Infomine (www.infomine.ucr.edu)

    - Librarians' Internet Index (www.ipl.org)

    - The Internet Archive (www.archive.org)

    - Resource Shelf (www.resourceshelf.com)

    - Project Gutenberg (www.gutenberg.org)

    - The National Academies Press (www.nap.edu)

    - Encyclopædia Britannica (www.britannica.com)

Other ideas for researching your field

- Sign up for Google AdWords and use the Keyword Tool. This will enable you to discover some of the words and phrases that people use to find information related to your topic. You'll also discover how much interest there is in these words and phrases and how many other websites target these words and phrases in their marketing.

- When you find interesting websites it's worth looking at the sites which 'backlink' to them. Backlinks are incoming links to a website or web page. Do a search on Google and you'll find tools which will help you find out which sites backlink to other sites.

- Read Blogs. A blog is a type of website where a person or a group voice their opinions and provide information about a particular topic. They tend to be updated more regularly than standard sites. You can search blogs via Google or a blog-specific search engine such as Technorati.

- Conducting an online survey is a good way to gauge public opinion or to carry out specific market research. It's normally pretty inexpensive to do. One tool that you could try is Survey Monkey (www.surveymonkey.com). Don't put survey takers off by asking too many questions. Limit yourself to 25 questions. Aim for the survey to take no more than seven minutes to complete.

- Visit social media websites such as Facebook, Google+ and Twitter. Carry out searches to see if you can find specialist groups on Facebook and Google+ related to your subject matter. Join them and see what people are discussing. Post comments and ask questions.

As you gather research material either print it off and file it in a folder, or save it in digital format on your computer.

Get eyeball to eyeball with the task

You should approach your research with an intense level of concentration. Bring all your focus to bear on it. Concentrate fully on this task in dedicated blocks of time. Eliminate distractions.

You're a special person these days if you can think about an idea for more than 15 minutes straight without a break. It's amazing how easily people are distracted in the modern world that we live in. There are so many external things and internal thoughts that compete for our attention.

The Pomodoro Technique is a very useful approach for improving your concentration levels.

- You work in 25 minute blocks. Either use an egg timer, a stop watch, a timer website or a smartphone app.

- Define what you'll work on in that time block. Only work on that task. If you finish the task in that time, great. Take a 5 minute break and then start another Pomodoro for another task.

- Take a 5 minute break when the timer goes off. Ideally walk away and do something different.

- Take a 20 minute break after you've done four Pomodoro sessions in a row.

The Pomodoro Technique is incredibly simple but it works for a number of reasons.

- 25 minutes is long enough for your brain to concentrate without tiring too much. If it's a task you hate then thinking that all you have to do is to spend 25 minutes doing it is not too daunting.

- It provides clarity. You define your task before you start each session. You know exactly what you'll work on.

- It lessens the temptation to multi-task.

- It provides you with mini-deadlines. Deadlines work and having one every 25 minutes makes it easy to stay on-task. After all, the next deadline is never that far away.

- It reduces internal interruptions and also imposes self-discipline.

Inspiration

Idea generation is not a question of dragging ideas out of your head. Your brain is not a library where you pull ideas out. You spark ideas by stimulating your brain. It feeds on stimulus. There are many ways of doing this.

Creativity is often the result of connecting things that didn't previously appear to be connected. You generate five times as many ideas when you stimulate your brain.

Think of the creative fields such as art, music and literature. An artist doesn't paint a carbon copy version of a landscape. That's what a photo is for. They use the scene as a stimulus. It inspires them to create their unique works of art.

Stimulus sets a chain reaction off in the brain. It's best to stimulate all your senses. Your brain is like a food processor. You need to feed it with raw material. And that's what the inspiration part of the Saturation step is all about.

Here are the best ways of stimulating and inspiring your brain as you're working on coming up with your Eureka Idea.

- Read material that is unrelated to your subject matter. Visit websites dedicated to topics that you have no interest in.
- Take some exercise. The best types are rhythmic, repetitive ones like running and swimming. It doesn't have to be a strenuous

pursuit, though. A brisk walk in the park is fine. Your brain represents just 2% of your body weight but uses 20% of your oxygen. Exercise feeds your brain with the feel-good chemicals and oxygen it needs to flourish. Exercise also gives you an interruption-free period of time to think.

- Take up a craft project, cook new meals or learn a new skill like a language. You should always be doing this. It's good for your creative brain to be stretched and exposed to new material and influences.

- Try writing a poem, a song or even a novel. The creative writing process places a discipline and a focus into your thinking.

- Travel and visit new places. Go to a museum or somewhere completely outside of your normal routine.

Input

It's very important to get an outside perspective on things. This part of the process is all about that.

Other people can give you support, insights, feedback, contacts, data, and information that you wouldn't otherwise receive by working on your own and flying solo.

You'll benefit considerably from getting a diverse range of input. It's good to hear from dreamers and people who are more factual in their approach.

Experience new people. Talk to people from different backgrounds and ages. They'll get you thinking in new and different ways. Old and young people are wonderful in this respect. These two groups are not asked what they think very often. Young people have a refreshing innocence and older people will have seen a lot in their lifetime and will tell it to you straight.

How to get outside input

The best way to talk through and get the thoughts of other people on your Ideation Task can be traced all the way back to ancient Greece. Socrates and his friends invented an approach to group conversations that they called Koinionia.

Koinonia is an ancient Greek term but no single English word is sufficient to describe its intensity and richness. It is derived from the word *koinos* which means common.

In essence, Koinonia is a complex and absorbing approach to building community or teamwork amongst people. Socrates and his colleagues took the word to mean 'spirit of fellowship'.

The Koinonia principles that Socrates and his contempories identified are as follows.

- *Dialogue.* In Greek, dialogue means 'to talk through' whereas discuss means 'dash to pieces'. They believed that the key to establishing dialogue was to exchange ideas without trying to change the other person's mind. The basic rules of dialogue are:
  - don't argue;
  - don't interrupt; and
  - listen carefully.
- *Clarify your thinking.* This means putting all your unproven beliefs

and assumptions to one side. This allows your thoughts to flow freely and creatively. You should remain unbiased.

- *Mutual respect.* This means treating every person as an equal. It means recognizing that everyone has something of equal importance to contribute. In a group situation each participant must be a full and active member of the group. No one person should be in control. You mustn't have anyone feeling as if they are of no use to the group because this will hinder open dialogue.

- *Be honest.* You should say what you think (without being rude) even if your thoughts are controversial.

It is widely agreed that the greatest physicist of all time was Albert Einstein. What is interesting is that, unlike many other physicists of his time, he was part of an extraordinary professional fellowship with three of his contemporaries.

Einstein, Werner Heisenberg, Wolfgang Pauli and Niels Bohr met up often and engaged in long, open and honest conversations about their work. In a large part, it was as a consequence of these dialogues that they each made the incredible scientific breakthroughs that marked their careers.

During their meetings they talked about ideas which later became the foundations of modern physics. They didn't conduct these conversations in a conventional way, however. They met in what you could call a spirit of fellowship.

In contrast, their contemporaries wasted their careers arguing over nuances of opinion and promoting their own ideas as being better than any others. They mistrusted their colleagues, covered up weaknesses and were reluctant to openly share their work. Many refused to discuss their thoughts about the problems because of fear of being labelled controversial by their colleagues. Others were afraid of being called ignorant. The majority of scientists of the time lived in an atmosphere of fear and politics. They produced nothing of significance.

"No two minds ever come together without, thereby, creating a third invisible, intangible force which may be likened to a third mind."
Napoleon Hill

Where are great ideas really born?

Does the image of a crazy genius working alone in search of a breakthrough idea come to your mind when you think about that question? It does for most people. If you go back through history you find that the vast majority of breakthrough ideas were the result of people working alone for a while but also together collaboratively in a group.

Collaboration causes creativity to spread. Flashes of inspiration fly faster and the insights are more profound when people collaborate together to generate new ideas. Breakthrough ideas tend to emerge over time as people have a series of ideas and insights which build on the ideas of others.

Innovations tend to be the result of a calm and collaborative process where:

- people build on other peoples' ideas in some way; or
- borrow ideas, tools or methods from other people.

When individuals do have a sudden flash of inspiration, you find that they are still part of something larger than themselves. For example, the Eureka moment that Archimedes had in the bathtub couldn't have come to him if he hadn't spent so many hours beforehand working alone but also talking and exchanging ideas with his fellow mathematicians and philosophers.

Groups that are too cohesive can be a problem as they can result in what is sometimes called groupthink. This is where group members try to minimize conflict and reach consensus by not critically testing, analysing, and evaluating the ideas of others.

Group creativity is about synergy which is defined as "the interaction of two or more agents or forces so that their combined effect is greater than the sum of their individual effects."

A healthy human body is an example of synergy at work. This is because it is a collection of subsystems working together and organised in a way that is mutually supportive of the whole. The body organs support each other and human life.

Again, you see this phenomenon in Nature all the time. For example, if you bring the flames of two candles together they don't create twice the amount of light. They create four times the quantity. The effect is exponential.

> **"*If I could solve all the problems myself, I would.*"** Thomas Edison

Crowd Creativity

When you think of people working in a group situation to come up with ideas does the word 'brainstorming' come to mind? Traditional brainstorming rarely works. It can actually be counterproductive.

One reason is that when people are in a face-to-face group situation they have a tendency to try to avoid conflict. People often have different views and, in order for the session to remain pleasant, they tend to go through social rituals so as not to upset one another.

They also have a tendency to slack off and do as much or as little work as the least productive person in the group. Also adults are often afraid of being embarrassed and so will hold back from suggesting 'crazy' ideas.

Importantly, the chances of a breakthrough idea being generated are increased when a large number of far-apart ideas, different perspective and life experiences are brought together. And you only get that in a group situation.

You might wonder why, if you're an expert in some area, why you would benefit from the ideas, perspectives and opinions of people from outside your field. It's because expertise can get in the way of and hinder the creative process.

Being too close to a problem can hamper you because if think you know the rules, what's been done before and what you think works and doesn't work, you rarely bother trying too hard for new ideas. According to Andrew Grove, the founder of Intel, the best way to solve a problem is to set aside what you already know.

Crowd Creativity is the answer to all of these issues. It is a way to build and manage a group of people in order to generate breakthrough ideas. The *Crowd Creativity* approach is based on the findings of academic research and genuine case histories.

Crowd Creativity is the set of 14 attitudes and aptitudes for connecting and coordinating brainpower that will enable any group of people to collaborate effectively in order to come up with a stream of original and valuable ideas.

The 14 principles are as follows:
- clarity
- diversity
- equality
- amiability
- impartiality
- unity
- honesty
- publicity
- community
- positivity
- originality
- fluidity
- fifty-fifty
- popularity

Clarity

Most people don't realise that their brain is an incredibly accurate and powerful goal-seeking mechanism. This ability lives deep in the subconscious mind. It resides below our radar of day-to-day awareness.

It is kicked into action when we are decisive and when we set precise goals. Our goal-seeking mechanism does not work when we are plagued with indecision and vague thinking. Make a resolution and give it clear and specific goals to aim at, however, and it responds by releasing a continuous flow of ideas and energy.

Diversity

We all have rigid, habitual ways of thinking. The brain is wired that way. The more times you think a thought, the more likely you are to think it again. If you need a new idea, you have to break that pattern. Diversity can do that for you.

Creativity works best when you have a varied group of people in terms of experiences and skills. New ideas often originate at the crossroads of different fields and cultures.

When you bring together ideas that have previously been perceived as completely separate, generating a multitude of new ideas becomes an effortless exercise. And to have great ideas you need to have lots of ideas.

Diversity fosters innovation, particularly ground-breaking innovation which is the type of innovation that businesses are desperate for.

Diverse groups are better at innovating. This is because new ideas are normally the result of combining existing ideas. But not all combinations of existing ideas offer the same value. Closely connected ideas that are combined tend to be unoriginal. Far-apart ideas when combined have the potential to be ground-breaking. Diverse groups are more likely to come up with unlikely combinations.

Diversity gives creativity an 'exponential shot in the arm'. If you look at creative societies and cultures, you'll notice that they are diverse. The reverse is also true. It's no coincidence that so many innovations and works of creativity come from countries such as the USA and the UK. They are melting pots.

Equality

Creativity is blocked when one person dominates, is arrogant, or thinks they cannot learn from others.

Often in business meetings and other group situations, one or more people dominate. Of course you need leadership so that the desired end result remains in focus and the rules are being followed. But you also need respect and full involvement.

We've all heard about the legend of King Arthur and his Knights of the Round Table, but, what you may not have heard suggested is that this legendary figure understood the importance of equality.

According to legend, Arthur's mission was to unify England and to promote peace and success. To do that, he assembled around him a group of the best and most well-mannered warriors in Europe.

He was determined not to make the same mistake as other Kings had made and took steps to prevent his team from becoming political, restless and power-crazy. He wanted them all to see themselves as equals with a voice that would be heard.

That is exactly what happened. Supported by Merlin and his Knights of the Round Table, King Arthur ruled justly and fairly. He righted wrongs, he risked great dangers yet he remained dignified and possessed great courage and insight. And he was able to do that because of the equality of the team he had around him.

The famous Round Table was significant too. It was both practical and symbolic. King Arthur dispensed with the traditional rectangular table favoured by other monarchs because he knew that if everyone sat around a round table then no position at the table would signify any greater importance than any other. He wanted his knights to talk to each other as equals.

Long, rectangular tables with the boss at the top inevitably create an uneasy atmosphere relating to status and pose practical problems of people, potentially, not being heard. Round or square tables do not present the same problem and make it easier to pool mental effort.

Amiability

The human mind cannot be creative when it feels threatened by people or situations. When faced with stressful circumstances the brain invariably switches the body into a state known as the 'fight or flight' mode.

This condition brings about a number of physical changes such as faster, shallower breathing. This response also alters the brain chemistry and hence thinking. People can become less rational and can find it difficult to think straight.

Confrontational situations and being in the company of bad-tempered people can bring on this primitive reaction and halt creativity. In contrast, amiable gatherings where people are being friendly, good-natured, sociable and agreeable can trigger creativity because people feel more comfortable proposing and discussing ideas.

Impartiality

For ideas to be created it is important to be unbiased and open to all possibilities. Bias is a fixed and closed state of mind where a particular viewpoint is held to be true.

Breakthroughs are often made when fixed points of view and assumptions are questioned because all ideas can be given a fair hearing.

Einstein questioned many of the assumptions which were firmly held by other physicists of his time. He was open to all possibilities and let his creative imagination go to work.

It also helps to suspend judgment, criticism and evaluation when new ideas are being generated. When hearing a new idea it can tempting to say, "Yes, *but*...." and to launch into a critical assessment and to 'knock down' the idea. Instead you should say, "Yes, *and*...." and come up with ways to build up the original idea.

Unity

People cooperate with each other when a group has 'oneness of mind'. As a consequence, people in the group soak up and amplify each other's creative powers. When thought power is blended in this way, magic happens.

A lot of people struggle with this concept because they either let their ego get in the way, or their social skills let them down. Studies indicate that 85% of someone's success in life comes down to their ability to behave in a positive and effective way with others.

The flow of ideas is extraordinary when a group is united. This is an advanced form of thinking. Everyone in the group will think bigger, faster and more inventively.

"In everyone's life, at some time, our inner fire goes out. It is then burst into flames by an encounter with another human being. We should all be thankful for those people who rekindle the inner spirit."
Albert Schweitzer

Honesty

You must see a problem as it really is if you are to solve it. If you don't you'll be solving the wrong problem. One of the Koinonia principles is honesty. People must feel free to say whatever is on their mind, but must do so in an agreeable way.

Publicity

You have to be prepared to air your ideas otherwise they cannot be added to by others. Most people are very protective of their ideas and fear that others will steal them. This fear exists if you have a 'scarcity mentality'.

There'll never be a world shortage of good ideas. If you believe that then you are misunderstanding how ideas work. All ideas are derived from ideas that have gone before them. They are combinations of other ideas. There can never be a shortage of ways in which ideas can be combined.

No idea that ever comes out of the head of any one person will ever be complete. So 'one-person generated' ideas will not work. They need input from other people.

So all new ideas must be put out there and publicised. That's not to say that sensible precautions should not be made to protect intellectual property, however.

Community

New ideas are fragile and can be killed at birth if they're not encouraged, supported and nourished.

Creativity is supported when people feel part of a distinctive group where the other members share similar interests, values or goals. This is particularly important when it comes to ideas. There are many psychological barriers associated with pursuing novel ideas. These include fear of failure and social rejection. When people feel part of a group of kindred spirits, the barriers can disappear.

We know that people are influenced by their surroundings. This is true for physical and 'virtual' environments. The single most important part of what is known as the 'suggestive environment' is the people with whom we routinely associate. This collection of people is often known as your reference group.

Dr David McClelland of Harvard University has studied the suggestive environment for decades. He is the author of the book The Achieving Society. In his research he has found that you can give a person first class training, but if that person is part of a negative group of people they will go back to their bad ways if they return to associating with that group.

"For every one of us that succeeds, it's because there's somebody there to show you the way out. The light doesn't always necessarily have to be in your family; for me it was teachers and school."
Oprah Winfrey

Positivity

Ultimately all ideas need to be evaluated. There's nothing at all negative about realism, looking for potential problems, looking for gaps and guessing at future consequences of an idea. But there is a sequence that must be followed. Evaluation should always come after the idea generation stage has fully run its course. Otherwise creativity will be stifled.

Whenever you hear an idea say, "What I like about that is …" and come up with something positive. The analytical part of our brain is often only too ready to jump in and judge. You need to give your creative side a chance to do its thing first. As all ideas are suggested they should be 'moved forward' in a constructive way.

The atmosphere of the group must be positive. Jealousy, negativity, envy, friction and lack of interest on the part of any member will bring progress to a halt so should be dealt with straightaway.

Originality

You want new, fresh ideas and independent thinking. This means you need to set things up so that group members are told that unique and valuable ideas are what is wanted. If you don't then there will be tendency for people to come up with ideas which are too obvious.

One of the things that we know from studies is that it helps if members try to generate ideas alone and also work together in a group on idea generation.

Fluidity

Research shows that a heightened state of mind which has been called 'flow' is essential to creativity. Flow can be achieved in a conversation if the following factors are in place.

- If the goal is clear.
- If thoughts are expressed freely and ideas are listened to fully.
- If people are comfortable talking about the subject matter and are engaged in the conversation.
- If there's feedback on the progress which is being made.
- If there is full concentration by all participants. This is a quality many people seem to have lost in the highly stimulated and distraction-rich modern world that we now live in. Concentrating means putting your attention fully on one aspect of the situation while ignoring all other things.

- Too much planning and too many rules tend to suffocate creativity and innovative problem solving. In contrast, spontaneity – although it is often inefficient – is far more likely to lead to better ideas and results. It's about improvising and the practice of creating 'in the moment' and in response to the stimulus of what's currently happening. This can result in the invention of new thoughts, practices, perspectives and new ways to act.

- It helps if people are exchanging ideas without trying to persuade other people of their value. In most conversations, people put a lot of energy into proposing and defending their ideas and point of view. When conversation participants give up on that and adopt a neutral standpoint, their energy can be devoted instead to creative lines of thought.

- Liquidity. Participants need to be open to conversations taking off in a new direction and should be willing to defer and go with the flow of the conversation.

- Participants should ask open questions. An open question is one in which no options for responses are given. "What are the possibilities?" is an example of an open question.

Fifty-fifty

Creativity doesn't work in a group situation if some people take and don't contribute. Sharing is about giving and receiving. It is one of Nature's laws because the world operates through a process of dynamic exchange.

Things don't work as they should if this law is flouted. For there to be a healthy balance in any environment, there needs to be an equal amount of giving and receiving over a period of time.

Sharing must also be unconditional. In other words, strings should not be attached to any giving.

Popularity

Groups are better than individuals at voting on and selecting ideas. After the idea generation phase has been completed, all ideas need to be tested and analysed based on the original definition of what was needed. Ideas need to be judged based on whether they are practical. Faults need to be found and corrected.

Studies show that groups are better at evaluating ideas than individuals. Individuals find it difficult to be emotionally detached from their ideas and the ideas of others.

> *"A person who can create ideas worthy of note is a person who has learned much from others."*
>
> Konosuke Matsushita

Master Mind groups

A perfect example of the Crowd Creativity principles in action are what are called Master Mind groups. Many exist today, but their origin dates back many years.

In 1908 a young man called Napoleon Hill was writing a series of articles about successful men. As part of his assignment he interviewed the industrialist Andrew Carnegie. At that time Carnegie was one of the most powerful men in the world. He told Hill that he believed that the process of success was a simple formula and he asked him if he would be prepared to interview over 500 successful men and women in order to identify the formula for success.

Hill went on to interview many of the most famous people of the time, including Thomas Edison, Alexander Graham Bell, George Eastman, Henry Ford, Elmer Gates, and John D. Rockefeller. The result was the million-selling book *Think and Grow Rich*.

Carnegie told Hill that he traced his own success to the 'sum total of the minds' of his business associates. He called this collective brain power a Master Mind.

Hill came to believe that a Master Mind was the secret to the success of all great men and women. He was quoted as saying that it was, "the very foundation stone of all outstanding personal achievements."

What Is a Master Mind?

Napoleon Hill defined the Master Mind as "a mind that is developed through the harmonious co-operation of two or more people who ally themselves for the purpose of accomplishing any given task."

He said that our minds are made of up of energy. When people meet up, the mind energies combine to form a 'third mind' which either results in positive or negative results.

A Master Mind produces good results and is formed when the group of people have positive energy, are in harmony with each other and share a definite aim. All the people in the group will have access to this Master Mind. Tapping into it provides inspiration and recharges the brains of all the individuals in the group. They can all contact and gather knowledge from the subconscious minds of all the other members of the group. This power becomes very noticeable because each person will have a more vivid imagination. They will all have the consciousness of what appears to be a sixth sense. It is through this sixth sense that new ideas will flash into the mind. Ideas related to the subject being discussed by the group will pour into the minds of the people present. The minds of those participating in the Master Mind become like magnets because they attract ideas and thought stimuli.

Who we associate with is important. It influences us in subtle ways. If you hang around with ambitious and positive people then you will find that you will become ambitious and positive as well. If you spend time with lazy and negative people then you will become influenced over time to be that way too.

The Inklings
The Inklings was a Master Mind group that consisted of great poets and writers such as C S Lewis, J R R Tolkien, Charles Williams, and Owen Barfield. They met each week for 30 years. They used to meet in Lewis' rooms at Magdalen College in Oxford on one evening and at a pub called The Eagle and Child on Tuesday mornings.

It was during these Master Mind meetings that literary classics such as *The Chronicles of Narnia* and *The Lord of the Rings* were refined and improved. Inklings members would read aloud from their most recent works. The other members would offer feedback and suggestions.

Lewis gave huge credit to his Master Mind group. He once said: "What I owe to them all is incalculable."

The Tennis Cabinet
Theodore Roosevelt became President of the United States at the age of just 42. He had a Master Mind group which he called his Tennis Cabinet. This was a group of old friends that he would play tennis with. They exercised their minds as well as their bodies by discussing and debating the pressing issues of the day.

The Junto
Benjamin Franklin formed a Master Mind Group of 12 members in 1727. It consisted of tradesmen, artists and craftsmen who were not welcome in elite circles of society. It lasted for more than 30 years. Some members formed spin-off groups.

The scientist, inventor, statesman, philosopher, musician and economist Benjamin Franklin also masterminded. He's famous these days as one of America's Founding Fathers and is regarded as one of that country's greatest ever citizens, but what is less well known is that he ran a Friday evening Master Mind club called Junto for many years.

It started in 1727 when he persuaded 12 of his friends to form an alliance committed to shared improvement. The group lasted for 40 years and ultimately became the core of the American Philosophical Society.

One of the things they did was to dream up publicly beneficial ideas. Projects they brought to fruition include the first library in the USA, a volunteer fire department, the first public hospital, police departments, paved streets and the University of Pennsylvania. Members suggested books, businesses, and friends to each other at Junto meetings.

The Vagabonds
One of the greatest of all Master Mind alliances was the one between Thomas Edison, Henry Ford, Harvey Firestone, the naturalist John Burroughs and the botanist Luther Burbank.

They were unlikely friends in many ways. Edison, Ford and Firestone were driven business people but John Burroughs was a famous author and naturalist whilst Luther Burbank was a scientist and botanist and developed over 800 strains and varieties of plants. They all shared something in common, though: they shared a sense of wonder, curiosity and the spirit of innovation.

They supported each other and, significantly, were the driving force that made each other accountable to make their dreams a reality.

Ford said this of his first meeting with Edison: "No man up to then had given me any encouragement. I had hoped that I was headed right. Sometimes I knew that I was, sometimes I only wondered, but here, all at once and out of a clear sky, the greatest inventive genius in the world (Edison) had given me complete approval. The man who knew most about electricity in the world had said that for the purpose, my gas motor was better than any electric motor could be."

The Chicago 6
This group was one of the most famous examples of the power
of the Master Mind principle. Two of the more famous members
were William Wrigley – he of Wrigley's chewing gum fame – and
John D Hertz.

When they formed in the early 1900s this group of half a dozen men
were all virtually penniless. They met for dinner every Saturday at a
local Chicago restaurant. They discussed their objectives for their
businesses and gave and received help in many forms. And after just
a few years each one was worth several millions of dollars. They
started their successful businesses with a great deal of help from
their Master Mind Group.

William Wrigley overcame near bankruptcy on several occasions and
was a pioneer in many ways. He was born in Philadelphia and he
moved to Chicago and founded the William Wrigley, Jr. Company
in 1891.

He blazed a trail by taking advantage of advertising methods that
were rarely used in his time such as print media. Plus he was one of
the first manufacturers to place products available for sale next to
cash registers. Today, the company he founded dominates the
market, with almost half the chewing gum sales in the United States.

John D Hertz is another example of huge achievement from humble
beginnings. He was born in Austria but emigrated to Chicago. He
founded the Yellow Cab Company and the Chicago Motor Coach
Company. Hertz ran the taxicab company until 1929, when he left to
found another rental car company, Hertz Rent-a-Car, which has since
grown to 6,500 locations with a fleet of over half a million vehicles.

Other examples

Dale Carnegie was a lecturer, author, and pioneer in the field of public speaking and the psychology of the successful personality. He said that he owed everything he ever achieved to the Master Mind principle.

Born into poverty in Missouri, at high school and college he was active in debating clubs. When he graduated he became a salesman and an actor. Eventually he went on to teach public speaking. He became an instant success with the hugely popular book *How to Win Friends and Influence People*.

There are some modern-day examples of people who used the Master Mind principle to achieve success. Bill Gates and Paul Allen pooled their collective brainpower to build Microsoft.

Also, for many years Michael Eisner, the ex-CEO of Disney, convened a Master Mind meeting of elite CEOs in Sun Valley, Idaho. Donald Trump also understands the power of many minds and has regularly brought together CEOs to leverage each other's success. Experience comes in two flavours, he says, yours and other peoples. It is foolish to ignore the experience of others.

Step 4
Technication

Having immersed yourself in the subject, stimulated your brain and sought input from other people, it is now time to work alone with your Ideation Task.

This next step in the process is about using a variety of creative thinking techniques. The approaches you will use at this step of the process will tap into your conscious mind. At step 5, you will harness your subconscious mind. The whole approach is called Colourful Thinking.

Colourful Thinking

One of the reasons why people aren't very good at coming up with valuable and original ideas is because they do not use their full range of thinking styles.

You need to vary the way that you think. We spend too much time thinking in a particular way. The type of thinking I'm referring to is fast-paced and fast-changing. We'll call this type of thinking 'chattering thinking'.

As a result we don't spend enough time thinking in other, quieter ways. Our brains are not meant to be in a constant state of stimulation. They are, though, with the hectic lifestyles that so many people live these days. It's no wonder that stress and anxiety are so common.

You wouldn't think that physically running around all day was a good idea, would you? It would be physically tiring and self-defeating. Yet most people think nothing of mentally running around all day. By the end of the day their brain has been run ragged. And we wonder why we feel so mentally drained for so much of the time?

The answer is what I call Colourful Thinking. This is where you use the full spectrum of your thinking styles ranging from the powerful and fast-paced way of thinking through to the slow and deep approach to thinking.

Your need to slow your brain down every so often

Think about what happens when you go on holiday. You not only physically rest but you also mentally give yourself a break. A holiday is 'time out' for your brain from the thoughts it engages in on a daily basis. Your brain gets a chance to slow down. From a thinking point of view it gets a change of scenery.

It's a good idea to calm down the pace of your thinking at more regular intervals in order to make the best use of your brain.

The brain is an electrochemical organ

Electricity is generated by the chemical reactions which occur in the brain. The electrical power created is very small, but it does occur in very specific ways. This electrical activity takes the form of brainwaves.

The brain produces different levels of electrical activity depending on the amount of information it needs to process. So if, for example, you are working on a detailed task, it lights up with electrical charges as it sends and receives lots of messages. While relaxed, it dimmers as its neurons are firing less often.

The four different types of brainwave patterns are as follows.

- Beta is the normal, awake consciousness associated with busy tasks.

- Alpha is the relaxed and reflective state that occurs during waking hours.

- Theta is a very relaxed state associated with coming out of or entering into a deep sleep. It is also the mental state associated with meditation.

- Delta is the state of mind when you are in a deep, dreamless sleep.

When you wake up in the morning from a deep sleep your brainwaves increase through the different frequencies. They increase from delta to theta and then to alpha and, finally, into beta. We then spend most of our day in beta.

We know from research that, although one brainwave state may dominate at any given time, the other brainwave states are always present at some level. So if you are in beta state whilst having a conversation with someone, alpha, theta and delta brainwaves still exist albeit at a low level.

Small children and animals function mainly at the theta, alpha and delta states. Adults operate mostly at beta.

Beta level brain activity relates to focusing on the outside world. Whereas alpha, delta and theta brainwaves correspond to focusing on the inner world.

Scientists have actually discovered a fifth brain wave called gamma (although there is some disagreement and some scientists do not distinguish beta from gamma waves). They are the fastest of the brainwave frequencies and are associated with peak concentration.

The four colours of thinking

Because of the time of day the four types of brainwaves normally occur at and the nature of the thoughts associated with each brainwave state, we can think of them as colours.

- Beta is DayTime thinking and the colour white.
- Alpha is DayDream thinking and the colour silver.
- Theta is DayBreak thinking and the colour yellow.
- Delta is NightTime thinking and the colour dark blue.

Brainwave Type	EEG (a measure of electrical activity in the brain)	Brainwave Frequency (cycles per second)	Type of thinking
Beta		14 - 40 cps	• Fully awake and alert • Generally associated with 'left brain' thinking activity
Alpha		8 - 13 cps	• Relaxed and calm • Daydreaming • Generally associated with 'right brain' activity • Meditation • Creative visualisation
Theta		4 - 7 cps	• Deeply relaxed • Deep meditation • Generally associated with 'right brain activity' • Access to insights, bursts of creative ideas and problem solving
Delta		0.5 - 3.5 cps	• Deep, dreamless sleep • Healing, regeneration and rejuvenation both mentally and physically

Nightime Thinking
delta brainwaves

Delta brainwave frequencies usually occur when you are in a deep sleep. NightTime thinking brainwaves are the slowest of the four. Interestingly, they are also the dominant brainwaves that babies experience in their first year of life.

At night, combinations and rearrangements of thoughts happen that would never occur to you while awake. Also, scientists have discovered that some frequencies within the delta range of 0.5 to 3.5 cycles per second help to set off growth and healing by the body.

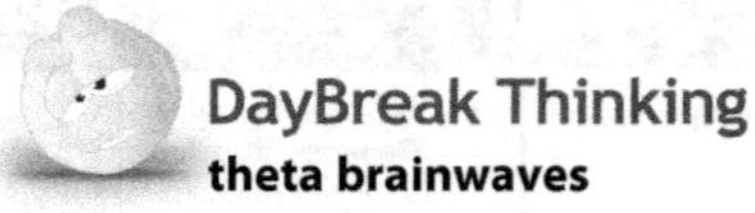

DayBreak Thinking
theta brainwaves

Theta brainwaves run at 6-10 cycles per second. The brainwaves are slower than alpha but faster than delta.

You'll most often be aware that your brain is operating at the theta brainwave level just as you wake up from a deep sleep. You're conscious but you feel relaxed and slightly dreamy and drowsy. Normally it only lasts a few minutes but you can train yourself to stay in theta for an extended period. You can train your brain to provide you with a free flow of creative ideas while in this mental state. This is also a great time to plan your day.

As an adult you will not usually enter the theta state again during the waking hours unless you consciously take action to relax deeply or meditate. Children under the age of 13 on the other hand, will often enter into this state of thinking during the day.

Your heart rate and your breathing slow down when you're in the theta thinking state.

Theta brainwave thinking is the sweet spot for many brain functions such as:

- intense creativity;

- enhanced learning;

- deep relaxation and stress reduction;

- extrasensory perception skills; and

- inspirational thoughts.

This is the state of mind that Thomas Edison called the twilight state. He trained himself to spend many hours at the theta level of thinking. He did this because he knew that ideas and solutions would come to him in this state of mind. Ideas that come to you in this state are often 'free flow' and are uncensored.

Daytime Thinking
beta brainwaves

Beta brainwave frequencies occur when you are fully conscious, awake and alert. They are the fastest of the four and operate when you have a lot of stimulation and things to do. They are associated with action and activity.

Beta brainwaves dominate the brain when you are awake, hence why I call it DayTime thinking. These brain waves are usually detected in the frontal lobes of the brain.

Beta brainwaves occur when your mind is strongly involved in something such as when you are:

- analysing problems;

- assessing situations;

- having conversations; and

- carrying out mental tasks.

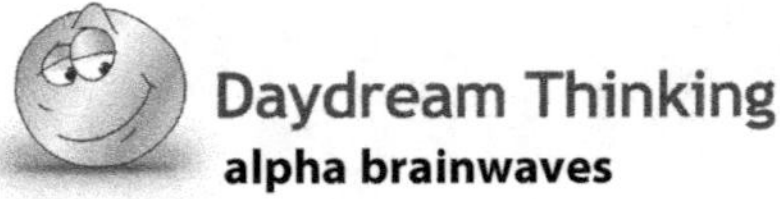 **Daydream Thinking**
alpha brainwaves

While at the alpha level, your mind is relaxed but you're still awake. Alpha brainwaves are not as frequent as beta but they are faster than theta. They are present when you daydream, relax or close your eyes.

You'll often enter an alpha brainwave state if you complete a task and then sit down afterwards to rest, relax and reflect. You'll also be thinking at the alpha level if you take a slow walk in the woods or around a park. You can also switch into an alpha brainwave state when you are doing repetitive tasks or ones that don't require much thought. For example, motorway driving or taking a shower. In other words, tasks that are so automatic that you can mentally disengage from them.

Alpha brainwaves enable you to be imaginative and access your intuition. They also allow you to reflect on, process and take in information.

The alpha state is ideal for:

- memorizing facts and data;

- performing complicated tasks;

- learning a language; and

- analysing problems or complex situations.

Colourful Thinking Techniques

Now you understand Colourful Thinking, it's time to start applying the four different thinking styles to the job of generating a Eureka Idea.

We'll start with DayTime thinking. Listed here are 18 idea generation techniques that utilize beta wave thinking. Pick half a dozen of the techniques at random and use them to come up with ideas in relation to your Ideation Task.

DayTime Thinking

You limit your ability to find answers if you assume too much about a problem. You get this with experts. It may seem counter-intuitive, but being an expert in a field can mean that you're less likely than a non-expert to come up with a creative idea in your specialist area.

The more of an expert you become in a subject, the more difficult it is to be innovative. This is because being an expert means you tend to specialise your thinking. You put borders around your thoughts. Often you fail to question things and investigate new possibilities. Non-experts do not have the expertise to draw borders so they look everywhere for ideas. History shows that breakthrough ideas in a particular field are often the brainchild of non-experts.

When you analyse the way you are thinking about a problem you'll almost certainly find that your thinking consists of a series of assumptions. An assumption is something that is taken for granted. It is not challenged because it is presumed to be fact.

By challenging your assumptions you can come up with new ideas.

Overturn-It is a technique where you find ideas by questioning your assumptions. You reverse them and see where that takes you in terms of new ideas. You even reverse assumptions that are so fundamental that they seem like they could not possibly be challenged.

The Overturn-It technique is useful if you're very stuck.

This is the process.

- Start by reading your Ideation Task Statement.

- List your assumptions about the problem.

- Reverse each one by writing down its exact opposite. These are your reversed assumptions.

- Think about how it might be possible to make the reversed assumptions happen.

- Record your thoughts and see what ideas emerge.

Mike Harris did this when he created First Direct, the UK's first telephone banking service. Until that point, the assumption had been that a bank needed a network of branches and would only be open for six hours on weekdays. First Direct reversed those assumptions by not having branches and by being open all year round on a 24/7 basis.

Cut 

Sometimes you may find that you become locked into only being able to think about a problem as a complete situation. This can be overwhelming. It can mean that you are unable to see the wood for the trees. So it can help to look at the individual parts of the problem one at a time.

There are many ways of cutting a problem or a situation up. Don't get too hung up on how you cut it into separate bits. For example, if you were trying to improve a product you might look at the individual parts separately.

This is the process.

- Start by reading your Ideation Task Statement.

- Look for ways that you can cut the problem into separate parts.

- Take each element one at a time and think of ways to change or improve it.

- Ask questions like:

  - "How else can this be done?"; and

  - "Why does this have to be this way?"

A few years ago the Dutch Boy paint company took this approach and improved one thing – the container. They put a handle on the side and one on the top. Plus they made the container plastic with a twist lid. Simple changes but they made a big difference to the ease-of-use of their product.

Quote IT!

This technique involves drawing on the ideas, inspiration and wisdom of the greatest thinkers of all time. Their thoughts can produce ideas and insights that will help with your situation or problem.

- Start by reading your Ideation Task Statement.

- Write down a list of people who, living or dead, appeal to you for whatever reason.

- Select one of these people and find a quotation from them. You'll find quotes listed at www.wikiquote.org.

- Reflect on the quotation.

- Write down your thoughts about it even if those thoughts apparently have nothing to do with your situation or problem. Writing in this way is sometimes known as a 'stream of consciousness'. It means 'a person's thoughts and conscious reactions to events, perceived as a continuous flow'.

- Choose the thought or combination of thoughts that appeal to you.

- Restate it in your own words.

- Then see if any ideas emerge in relation to your challenge.

Let's work through an example and we'll use the social network I have created for Ideas People which is called The Ideas Crowd (www.ideascrowd.com).

My Ideation Task Statement is as follows.

The Problem: The site has just launched and the first milestone of 1,000 'raving fans' has not yet been reached.

The Purpose: The Ideas Crowd will grow exponentially and become more valuable to its members when the first milestone is achieved. This is because the raving fans will help to spread the word through word of mouth. So it is important to reach this critical mass point.

The Question: In what ways can I market The Ideas Crowd so that it has a membership of 1,000 raving fan as soon as possible?

I selected Aristotle and a quotation that appeals which is:

"He who has overcome his fears will truly be free."

So my next task was to write down whatever thoughts occurred to me as a result of reflecting on that quote. This is what I came up with.

> *We're caged in by our fears. They stop us from doing what we want to do. We are trapped. It's like we're stuck in a virtual prison. We need to find the key or some other way to get out. Either that or serve our time in the prison until our sentence is up. A prisoner has time to think when they're locked away. They should come out a better person. A free person is someone who has learned their lessons. It's scary. It takes courage to conquer your fears. But we have courage. Our ideas are like that as well. They're held prisoner by our fears. We need to let them free. They will flourish*

when they're not held back. They will fly if they're good enough. They're like a virus. If the concept for The Ideas Crowd is good enough then word will spread about it. Ideas People will become courageous about their ideas if they have somewhere they can hang out together. They will release their fears.

This is exactly as I wrote it. I did not edit my thoughts. I just wrote down whatever came out of my head. I then tried to relate these thoughts to my Ideation Task question and the following ideas occurred to me.

- Potential members might have a few fears so I should take measures to overcome them.
- For example, some potential members might be concerned that they would not get value for money. So how about providing a money-back guarantee?

- Some members might be concerned about sharing their ideas. A few solutions came to mind to overcome that issue. One is a set of rules that all members have to sign up to which stipulate that members should support and not ridicule the ideas of others and should build on and not take the ideas of others. Another solution is to explain on the home page that ideas can only be improved by sharing them with others.

- I recognised that there is a value in the support that comes from being part a group of people that share your talents and values. The idea I had is to market the fact that members will be part of a large and virtual Master Mind group. Via the site, they will also be able to form sub-groups that can serve as smaller Master Mind groups or project groups.

- Having a hangout is useful so the idea is to go to the online and offline places where Ideas People hangout currently, such as Facebook and trade bodies, and persuade them of the merits of joining a community of very kindred spirits.

Split IT!

Ideas often come from combining separate elements in new ways. This technique involves doing just that.

- Start by reading your Ideation Task Statement.

- The first step is to get to the essence of a problem. You're trying to summarise it in two words. Or put another way, come up with two words that state the essence of your challenge. Don't worry too much about the correctness of the split.

- So if we take an example. Let's say we have a family opticians practice which wants to increase its number of clients.

- So we split the challenge into two separate units – 'family' and 'opticians'.

- The next step is to split each word into two more attributes.

  - So we could split 'family' into 'adults' and 'children' and we could split 'opticians' into 'eye tests' and 'products'.

  - If you split 'adults' you might get 'working age adults' and 'retired adults'.

  - Split 'children' and you might get 'junior school age' and 'secondary school age'.

  - Split 'eye tests' and you might get 'free' and 'specialist'.

  - Split 'products' and you might get 'contact lenses' and 'spectacles'.

- Continue to split each word until you feel you have enough to work with.

- Now examine each word for ideas. Try mixing and matching the words to see if that triggers new ideas. Mixing and matching will give you all kinds of ideas that you might not have thought of – how about a marketing campaign aimed at offering free eye tests to retired people?

I took The Ideas Crowd challenge mentioned earlier and used the Split-It technique.

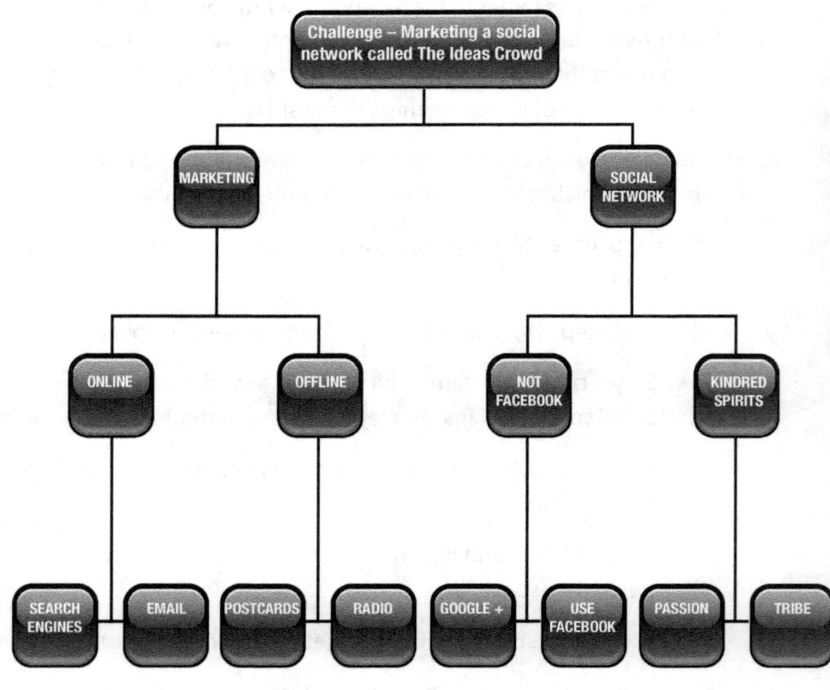

Ideas that came from this exercise were as follows.

One of the best ways of finding people who are likely to be interested in a specialist social network is via groups and fanpages on other social networks such as Facebook, Google+, and LinkedIn. After all, these people are already familiar with what social networks are and how they work.

Another idea that occurred to me is the tribe analogy. One definition of a tribe is 'a group of families that have a leader and work in a community'. Another is 'a social division in a traditional society consisting of families or communities linked by social, economic, religious, or blood ties, with a common culture and dialect, typically having a recognized leader'. A third definition I found is that a tribe is 'a group of people connected to an idea, connected to a leader and connected to each other'.

If people are connected to an idea the obvious question is: What is the 'big idea' they want to be connected to? People join a tribe because they want to be associated with something bigger than themselves.

This triggered a few ideas.

- If I use the tribe analogy for The Ideas Crowd, then it needs a leader. And so it became clear to me that my role must become the 'leader of the tribe'.

- How about the concept of The Ideas Crowd being a place where the tribes' people work? So the idea is that the service is positioned as, not just a virtual location where Ideas People come to meet each other, but also a place where they get their idea generation work done.

- The tribe analogy also triggered another thought for me. By connecting tribe members with each other you increase their enthusiasm about the tribe. And by giving them a voice in its development, they get a sense of ownership and they will want to invite like-minded people they know to join.

Map

We don't think in straight lines. But, as a society, we've developed the habit over the years of writing in a linear way. We write across and down the page.

This approach means that it's very difficult to make connections between the things we have written. But ideas are often the result of making connections between our various thoughts. Writing your thoughts and ideas in the form of a mind map helps you to make connections. New ideas will emerge as you create and review your mind map.

The Map-It technique involves drawing a mind map centred on the Eureka Idea you are seeking. A mind map is a diagram which represents words, ideas and other items arranged around a central key word or idea.

- Start by reading your Ideation Task Statement.

- Put a word or a short phrase in the centre of your mind map. This central thought should encapsulate the essence of your Ideation Task Statement.

- As new ideas, information and thoughts come to mind write them down on branches radiating out either from the centre or from other branches. Don't use lots of words to express these ideas. Ideally condense the thought into one word or just a few.

- Look for relationships. Use lines, colours, arrows and branches as you see connections between your ideas.

- Draw quickly on blank paper without pausing, judging or editing. You can modify it later. For now, just get the ideas down as they occur to you.

- Make your mind map colourful. Add pictures as well.

- New ideas will occur to you as you work on and review your ideas mind map.

The original proponent of mind maps in general is Tony Buzan. Visit his website if you'd like to find out more about mind maps – www.thinkbuzan.com. From there you can also purchase iMindMap, his excellent mind mapping software program.

Question IT!

This technique involves asking a series of questions. What you're trying to do is to look for ways of changing something and seeing what ideas emerge from doing that.

- Start by reading your Ideation Task Statement.
- Then seek answers to these nine questions:
    - What can be substituted?
    - What can be combined?
    - What can I adapt or copy from something else?
    - What can be modified?
    - What other use can it be put to?
    - What can be removed or stopped?
    - What can be reversed?
    - What can be rearranged?

Contest It!

There are normally positive and negative aspects to any problematic situation. To find a solution it helps to become aware of what these aspects are.

With the Contest-It technique you plot the positive and negative forces in the situation. Your aim is to then maximize the positives and to minimize the negatives.

- Start by reading your Ideation Task Statement.

- Describe the best- and worst-case scenarios.

- List the conditions of the situation. These are the things that you regard as essential to solving the problem.

- Notice the tug-of-war which is taking place. By listing the conditions you will be able to work out which forces are pulling you towards the best- and the worst-case scenarios. Think of what you need to do to make the best-case scenario happen.

The things that you can do to make the best-case scenario happen are to:

- strengthen the positive aspects of the situation;

- reframe the negative aspects into problems that need to be solved; and

- add more positives.

Box It!

New ideas are often the result of combining things. This technique gets you to think about new combinations.

With the Box-It technique you break the thing in question down into its individual attributes and then build it up again by recombining certain attributes.

- Start by reading your Ideation Task Statement.
- Select the attributes of the challenge.
- List as many variations as you wish for each attribute.
- Try different combinations of attributes and variations to create entirely new ideas.

Let's say, for example, that you are a tableware manufacturer and that you decide that you want an idea for a new bowl.

Let's take the attributes of a bowl to be 'usage', 'material' and 'features' and list some of the variations for those attributes.

Use	Material made from	Features
Cereal	Acrylic	Coloured
Dessert	Ceramic	Small
Dinner	Glass	Large
Fruit	Melamine	Children's
Noodle	Porcelain	Rimmed
Pasta	Stoneware	Heart shaped
Rice	Copper	Contemporary
Salad	Wooden	Square
Serving		Modern
Soup		Hand Painted
		Rectangular
		Straight Sided

Of course there are more variations that could be listed, particularly as far as features are concerned. But if we take this list and start looking for combinations of variations you'll see how new ideas can form.

- How about a salad bowl for children that is heart shaped and made of acrylic?

- Or what about a soup bowl made out of porcelain that is rectangular in shape?

On some occasions the combinations you come up with will make for good ideas. On other occasions the combinations themselves will not be good ones but they may spark other original and valuable ideas.

Layer IT!

You can sometimes get an answer to a problem by writing down whatever random thoughts or observations occur to you about the situation. You then reflect on what you've written.

- Start by reading your Ideation Task Statement.

- Now write down between six and eight sentences that occur to you when you think about it. Make them complete sentences.

- The statements do not need to be connected or follow on from each other. The sentences can be random. You don't have to try to write down statements which cover all aspects of the situation, either.

- Now read the statements – the layers as I call them – and quietly reflect on them.

- Let ideas form as a result of this reflection.

Working on The Ideas Crowd question mentioned earlier I came up with the following list when I used this technique.

Many people who I have classified under the term 'Ideas People' probably don't use that term when they think about themselves and the work they do. So the use of that term probably needs to be explained clearly on the site.

Great ideas can spread rapidly these days because of social media and the Internet in general.

Ideas People come from a wide variety of fields which is good because you need diversity.

It would be excellent if I could get the endorsement of an expert in the field such as Seth Godin.

The Ideas Crowd must stand out in some way.

It must be remarkable in both senses of the word. That is, it must be outstanding and it must be something that people want to talk about both online and offline.

As you can see, the sentences do not comprehensively cover every aspect of the challenge. They are complete sentences and I wrote them down in the order in which they occurred to me. I did not edit them in any way.

Out of this exercise came a few marketing ideas.

- Seek the endorsement of the service by a respected figure.

- The importance of positioning the service so that it is unique and stands out from the crowd.

- Ensure the nature of the service is such that it gets talked about and attracts publicity.

Position IT!

If you're trying to spot a new opportunity in a particular market it helps to see how existing products and services in that market are positioned in relation to each other.

- Start by reading your Ideation Task Statement.

- Draw a grid with four boxes. Label the four areas as follows.
    - *High involvement* – this is for products and services where the customer spends a lot of time, thought, energy and other resources in making the purchase decision.

    - *Low involvement* – this is for products and services where the customer doesn't spend a lot of time, thought, energy and other resources in making the purchase decision.

    - *Think* – this is for where people buy based mainly on reason, logic and prudence.

    - *Feel* – this is for where people buy based mainly on emotion, impulse, desire and passion.

- Place each existing product or service which is on sale in the market in the grid that you think it belongs.

- The Position-It grid now makes it very easy for you to see the potential gaps in the market. So new product or service ideas can be spotted at a glance. This approach also helps you to come up with advertising ideas.

Look at how Apple positions its products in the marketplace. Prior to Apple's arrival on the scene, the computer market was dominated by companies selling products that you would position in the 'high involvement/think' square of the grid.

Apple didn't want to go head-to-head with the likes of IBM so they decided to aim at the 'feel' side of the grid. They decided to make a computer that was for ordinary people and not experts. They also made their computers look wonderful. They weren't just boring grey boxes.

Apple did the same in the MP3 player market with the iPod and in the tablet computer market when they launched the iPad. Both the iPod and the iPad look great and are very easy to use.

Interrogate IT!

Many people avoid thorough and intense thinking. It's hard work and, when faced with a problem, it can be tempting to just jump in and start guessing. It pays dividends to ask the right questions and not stop until you get the answers.

Interrogate-It is a technique where you systematically work through a checklist of problem-solving questions. It guides your thinking and can lead to an answer.

This particular set of questions was developed by the CIA to enable their agents and operatives to think about a problem thoroughly.

- Start by reading your Ideation Task Statement.
- Work through the checklist of questions, which are listed below.
  - Why is it necessary to solve the problem?
  - What benefits will you gain by solving the problem?
  - What is the unknown?
  - What is it you don't yet understand?
  - What is the information you have?

- What isn't the problem?

- Is the information sufficient? Insufficient? Redundant? Contradictory? Should you draw a diagram of the problem? A figure?

- Where are the boundaries of the problem?

- Can you separate the various parts of the problem? Can you write them down? What are the relationships of the various parts of the problem?

- What are the constants (things that can't be changed) of the problem?

- Can you solve the whole problem? Part of the problem?

- What would you like the resolution to be? Can you picture it?

- How much of the unknown can you determine?

- Can you derive something useful from the information you have?

- Have you used all the information?

- Have you taken into account all essential notions in the problem?

- Can you separate the steps in the problem-solving process? Can you determine the correctness of each step?

- Can you see the result? How many different kinds of results can you see?

- How many different ways have you tried to solve the problem?

- What have others done?

- Can you intuit the solution? Can you check the result?

- What should be done? How should it be done?

- Where should it be done?

- When should it be done?

- Who should do it?

- What do you need to do at this time?

- Who will be responsible for what?

- Can you use this problem to solve some other problem?

- What is the unique set of qualities that makes this problem what it is and none other?

- What milestones can best mark your progress?

- How will you know when you are successful?

Random IT!

Often we get locked into a particular way of thinking. It can be difficult to break out of that in order to come up with new ideas.

Random-It is technique for doing that. What you do is to connect issues which are unrelated to one another. In so doing, you will generate new ideas.

The field of modern art is an example of where putting things together which are not related is quite common.

The Random-It technique opens up your thinking.

- Start by reading your Ideation Task Statement.

- What you need is do is to obtain a random word that has no connection with the problem or situation you are working on. This random word will spark fresh ideas.

- The best random words are ones which are simple and visual.

You'll find websites that will generate a random word for you. This is one example – www.goo.gl/x9GJ9

- Think about your random word and write down any thoughts that the word brings to mind for you. Another phrase for what you do at this point is free association. This means to spontaneously think of any words, ideas, emotions, and feelings that come to mind when you think about the word. Think of as many as you can.

- Use the word given. Don't keep seeking a new random word.

- Now reflect on your Ideation Task Statement. Do any of the thoughts you've just come up with help you? Force a connection between your thoughts about the random word and your challenge.

- What new ideas do doing this spark?

Taking the Ideas Crowd example again, I took the random word 'frog'. When I free associated on that word I came up with the following list.

Jump, ribbet, googly eyed, frog's legs, France, tadpole, Freddo (a brand of chocolate bar in the UK), green, jump, hop, pond and Kermit.

When I forced a connection between these words and the challenge I came up with the following ideas.

- I was intrigued by the word jump so I went online to see what I could find out the jumping ability of frogs. They are generally recognized as exceptional jumpers. For example, the Australian rocket frog, Litoria nasuta, can leap over 50 times its body length (5.5 cm), resulting in jumps of over 2 meters. Apparently the acceleration of the jump may be up to twice gravity. Connecting this to the challenge, the idea that occurred to me is the fact that members of The Ideas Crowd can jump-start and accelerate their ideas and their careers by being an active participant. This is a powerful marketing message.

- I was also interested in the word 'tadpole'. Again I went online to find that the life cycle of frogs consists of four main stages: egg, tadpole, metamorphosis and adult. And that is not unlike the life cycle that ideas go through. The idea that occurred to me was that I could use that metaphor in the marketing. That is, when you first have an idea it is like an egg. It is not yet fully formed but it has potential. The egg then becomes a tadpole but is still highly vulnerable as are most new ideas. Metamorphosis is where the tadpole changes its form and frog is the adult stage. Ideas often go through a similar process as they evolve into their final, mature form.

"Keep on the lookout for novel ideas that others have used successfully. Your idea has to be original only in its adaptation to the problem you're working on."
Thomas Alva Edison

Analogy IT!

An analogy is where you make a comparison between two separate things. The Analogy-It technique involves comparing something similar from an unrelated area to the challenge you are working on.

- Start by reading your Ideation Task Statement.

- Then research a few fields that have nothing to do with your own.

- Are there similar problems? Have they been solved? If so, could a solution be adapted to your problem?

One place to look for analogies is Mother Nature. If you look for a connection between your challenge and something similar in Nature you might find the answer. For example, the helicopter was invented based on the way that a humming bird flies.

Let's work through an example and again we'll use the social network I have created for Ideas People. It occurred to me that The Ideas Crowd is analogous to the Master Mind groups that were created by people like Abraham Lincoln.

Ideas from these forerunners that could be incorporated into The Ideas Crowd are as follows.

- Drawing on how *Junto* worked, how about having ideation tasks that the whole membership can work on such as challenges to dream up publicly beneficial ideas?

- The technology obviously didn't exist so the early Master Mind groups could only meet face-to-face. There is huge value in meeting in-person so how about adding in the facility whereby Ideas Crowd members can organise local events?

Mindstorm IT!

One of the reasons why people often feel so stressed is that they keep so much stuff in their heads. Holding onto thoughts and ideas is tiring. Plus, a great idea could be amongst all those thoughts kicking around in your head.

The Mindstorm-It technique draws all those thoughts out into the open.

- Start by reading your Ideation Task Statement.

- Sit quietly for a while and then start writing.

- Write down everything that comes to mind on a piece of paper. Write each of the thoughts and ideas down in as concrete a form as is possible. Number each idea or thought.

- Keep writing until you get to at least 25. Keep writing down thoughts and ideas beyond 25 if they keep occurring to you.

- Pick one of the ideas and put it into practice immediately. Acting on your ideas encourages your brain to keep providing you with great ideas.

Roulette IT!

This technique involves generating ideas by forcing a connection between common attributes and your challenge. It's excellent for generating new ideas.

- Start by reading your Ideation Task Statement.

- Draw a circle and number it like a clock (1 to 12).

- Write down 12 attributes or aspects of the subject of your challenge. Assign each aspect to a number.

- Throw a die to choose the first attribute to think about.

- Throw two dice to choose the second attribute.

- Think about the first attribute. Free associate in relation to it. In other words, write down a list of any words that come back to mind when you think about it.

- Write a second list which is your free associations in relation to the second attribute.

- Look at both of your lists and free associate based on both of your lists.

- Search for a link between your free associations and your challenge.

Let's work on an example. Imagine you want to come up with an idea for a new product or service for children that involves toys.

The 12 attributes could be types of toys:

1. Action figures
2. Animals
3. Dolls
4. Dressing up gear
5. Arts and crafts
6. Games
7. Puzzles
8. Science-based toys
9. Musical instruments
10. Vehicles
11. Sports
12. Weapons

I rolled one die and got 4 and rolled two dice and got 6.

So first of all I free associated on 'dressing up gear' and came up with the following list.

> *Cowboys and Indians, fancy dress parties, make up, props, costumes, Halloween, joke shops.*

Next I free associated on the word 'games' and came up with the following list.

> *Monopoly, KerPlunk, chess, Subbuteo, iPhone apps, Wii, PlayStation, Lego, dominoes, hopscotch.*

The next step is to play around with the lists.

- How about a Wii game modelled on the Cowboys and Indians role play game?

- Or what taking the Halloween concept and applying it to Lego? So how about creating a series of scary Lego sets which could include haunted houses?

Diagram IT!

Sometimes the issue is the opposite of the one faced with the Cut-It technique. In other words, sometimes we struggle to see the bigger picture. We only see what is immediately around us. Diagram-It is a technique which helps you to see the bigger picture. It helps you to see the relationship between the various aspects of the situation.

You diagram the obstacles in a particular way and use this information to find the answers. The shape of the diagram forces you to cluster the issues around the central idea. Themes will emerge as you work through this process.

It shifts your thinking from looking at a narrow snapshot of the issue to a broader perspective where you can better see relationships and connections.

- Start by reading your Ideation Task Statement.

- Draw the diagram shown and write the problem or central idea at the centre.

- Write the main aspects or themes of the situation in the circles surrounding the centre. Keep it to 6 to 8 themes.

- Use the ideas written in the circles as the central themes for the surrounding boxes.

- Continue the process until the diagram is complete.

- Notice the ideas which emerge as you do this.

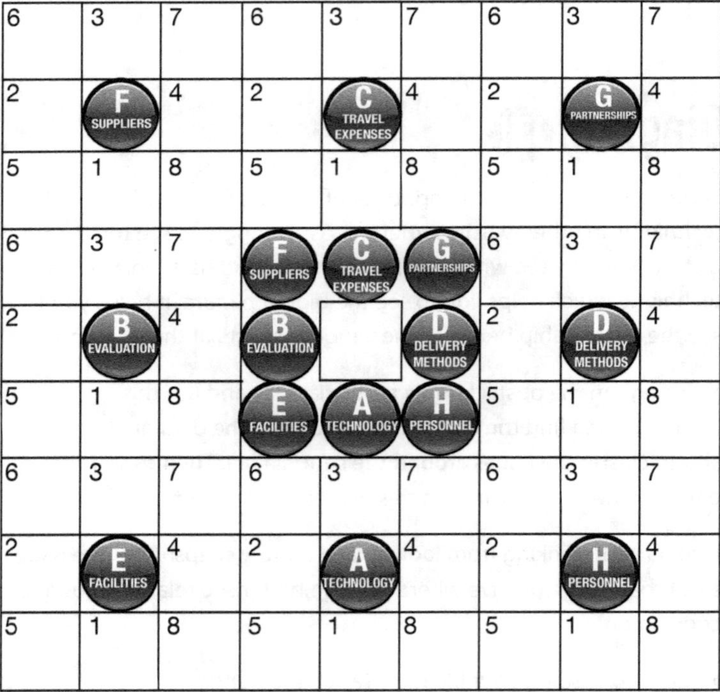

So with the example we've been using of marketing The Ideas Crowd the diagram could start out like this.

Then for each of eight circles I did the same thing. So the themes for the 'Converting Prospects' circle shaped up like this.

I did this for each of the eight circles. One of the ideas that occurred to me as a result of this exercise was to do Split A/B testing of the sales copy and visuals. Because I saw the complete picture from the using the Diagram-It technique I was able to spot gaps in my previous thinking.

Graphic IT!

Before the written word was invented we communicated by using pictures and symbols. Visual thinking and forms of communication are still very effective.

- Start by reading your Ideation Task Statement.

- Divide the challenge into its separate aspects.

- Draw a graphic symbol on an index card to depict each aspect.

- Place all the cards on a table with the graphic symbols facing up. Move them around looking for relationships.

- Look at the cards and see if any ideas emerge.

System IT!

This technique takes a very systematic approach to solving the challenge. The basis for this technique is to look for the causes and to find ways of fixing them.

- Start by reading your Ideation Task Statement.

- Write down all the possible causes of the problem.

- Write down all the possible solutions which will address the causes and will fix the problem.

- Be decisive and pick one solution.

- Set a deadline for when you will implement the solution.

- Take the necessary action on that day.

Step 5
Gestation

So far you've been thinking hard about the problem. DayTime Thinking is tiring. Now it's time to give the rational and logical left hemisphere of your brain a break. You've racked your brain and now it's time to reset it and then relax it.

You're now going to stop thinking about your Ideation Task in a conscious way. You're going to be handing it over to the other sides of your thinking.

Professor Stellan Ohlsson from the University of Illinois at Chicago has studied the Eureka moment. He says that when all conscious attempts to solve a problem have failed your brain becomes deadlocked. You become frustrated.

Ohlsson believes that this impasse can cause unconscious processes within the brain to then kick in. When this happens the brain changes the way that it sees the problem. This can act as a trigger for it to come up with a Eureka Idea.

This is the step in the process where you switch from using your conscious mind to using your subconscious mind and to accessing the superconscious mind.

You will start using use DayDream, DayBreak and NightTime thinking techniques. Pick two or three of the DayDream techniques at random to do, plus do the DayBreak and the NightTime technique. Use them to come up with ideas in relation to your Ideation Task.

Intuition

We are all intuitive. Intuition is like any other skill. The more you practice it, the better you'll get at it.

There is a simple way to practice tapping into your intuitive abilities. All you need to do is make a habit of guessing how future situations will turn out. You'll get better at it with practice.

It also helps to become tuned into intuitive impulses each day. Your intuition is talking to you all the time. Listen in closely. Your intuitive voice is quiet. How do your intuitions feel? When do they occur?

Here are some clues as to when your intuition is at work.

- When you feel you know how to solve a problem but you have no idea how you know.

- When you see how a solution from an unrelated problem links to your current problem.

- When you recognise the crux of a problem.

- When you identify a solution based on the fact that it 'feels right'.

Beta brain waves dominate your thinking while you're awake and going through your day. Alpha brain waves are always present but they're quieter. For this reason they are normally overwhelmed by the active and intense beta brain wave pattern.

Think of it like this. Stars can be seen in the night sky. They're still there during the day but cannot be seen because the sun outshines them or the clouds cover them.

Alpha wave thinking can help you to spot a solution that is there but you cannot see. Think of this as clearing your mind.

You'll either slip into alpha wave thinking on your own – for example, by going for a walk – or you can take yourself into that state of mind through a technique.

Alpha wave thinking is promoted by four simple things.

- A quiet environment, whether indoors or outdoors.
- A specific mental technique for relaxation.
- A passive attitude – empty your mind, do not dwell on thoughts.
- A comfortable position, one that will allow you to meditate without sleeping.

Imagination

As kids we used our imagination all the time. We'd ask ourselves questions such as:

- What if?
- Just suppose?

It is possible to recapture your imagination. That talent is still there. You just haven't used it very much recently.

DayDream Thinking

Chill IT!

This is a deep breathing technique which relaxes your body and your mind.

The important point is to breathe deeply from your abdomen. This means that you'll get as much fresh air as possible into your lungs. You inhale more oxygen when you take deep breaths from your abdomen than you do when you take shallow breaths from your upper chest. The extra oxygen means you that you feel less tense, short of breath and anxious.

- Sit comfortably with your back straight.

- Put one hand on your chest. Put your other hand on your stomach.

- Breathe in through your nose so that the hand on your stomach rises. The hand on your chest should not move very much at all.

- Count slowly and breathe out through your mouth. Exhale as much air as you can while contracting your abdominal muscles. The hand on your stomach should move in as you exhale. Your other hand should move very little.

- Notice the thoughts and ideas which pop into your mind when you reach the point of being fully relaxed.

Intuit 

This technique allows you to tune into your intuition.

- Sit down in a quiet place with a notepad and pen. Make sure you won't be disturbed.

- When you feel relaxed, read your Ideation Task Statement.

- Think about it quietly it for a few minutes.

- Write down appropriate questions on your notepad. For example:

  - What is best?

  - What should I do?

- Wait for any answers that pop into your head. Write down the answers as they come to mind without analysing them.

- Keep writing down further questions as they occur to you. Write down those answers as they occur to you.

- Look at your notes when you feel like you have finished asking any further questions. Intuitive answers may well be there. You'll instinctively know what is intuitive and what is not.

Imagine IT!

This is a technique where you ask yourself a series of fantasy questions. This gets your brain to think about possibilities. You let your mind get playful and kick around crazy ideas. This fuels your imagination and can trigger ideas.

- Sit down in a quiet place with a notepad and pen. Make sure you won't be disturbed.

- When you feel relaxed, read your Ideation Task Statement.

- Write down a whole series of 'what if' questions related to your challenge. For example, let's say you're trying to think of a new type of soft drink. 'What if' fantasy questions could include:

  - What if there was a sensor on the can and it could only be opened if it recorded that you were thirsty?

  - What if you could choose how many bubbles there were in your drink?

  - What if the Government ordered that all soft drinks had to be sold in containers made of wood?

- Attempt to answer the questions.

- Notice what ideas emerge.

Draw It!

An effective way to solve a problem you've become bogged down with is to shut down your logical brain for a while and to use a technique called Draw-It.

Drawing is a right-brain activity. It works because we think in terms of pictures as well as words. It, therefore, follows that we can solve problems using pictures as well as with words.

The Draw-It technique involves using freehand scribbling, doodling and drawing to inspire ideas.

- Sit down in a quiet place with a notepad and a selection of pencils and pens. Make sure you won't be disturbed.

- When you feel relaxed, read your Ideation Task Statement.

- Then sit quietly until images, scenes or symbols that represent your situation come into your mind.

- Draw as your mind wants you to draw. Don't worry about how it looks. Just draw. Use freehand scribbling, doodling and standard drawing.

- Do as many drawings as you need.

- Examine your drawing or drawings and write down what comes to mind. First write down the individual words or phrases that occur to you. Understanding your drawings is like untying a knot. It draws you back to your subconscious mind, which is where the drawing started.

- Then write a paragraph based on these words or phrases.

- Finally, think about how it all relate to your challenge or problem. What ideas come to mind?

Solitude

Rarely do we ever sit and do nothing for prolonged periods of time. Except maybe when we go on holiday.

Doing nothing allows your mind to clear. It allows your brain to switch from beta to alpha brain wave thinking which, of course, means that ideas can emerge from your subconscious.

- The idea is to sit quietly doing nothing in a place where you won't be disturbed for 30 to 60 minutes.

- Sit down in a quiet place with a notepad and a pen. Make sure you won't be distracted by any gadgets such as your computer or the phone.

- You'll probably fidget initially. You'll probably be tempted to get up and do something. An urgent item from your 'to do list' might pop into your head. Leave yourself a reminder note but don't be tempted to stop and do the task. You must resist that urge.

- After about 20 to 25 minutes your brain and your body will settle down. That's when ideas will flow.

"If you are seeking creative ideas, go out walking. Angels whisper to a man when he goes for a walk." *Raymond Inmon*

Nature IT!

In a sense, this technique is like taking your problem for a walk in Nature. We're at our best when we're in Nature. It's where we're meant to be. Notice how relaxed you feel when you go for a walk along the beach or alongside a river.

- Go for a walk for 30 to 60 minutes.
- Walk slowly.
- Notice your surroundings using all your senses.
- After about 20 to 25 minutes your brain and your body will settle down.
- That's when ideas will flow.

"Me thinks that the moment my legs begin to move, my thoughts begin to flow."
Henry David Thoreau

Mirror IT!

This is an excellent technique if you know what a solution to problem looks like, but don't yet know how to get there.

- Use the Chill-It relaxation technique to get yourself to an alpha brain wave state.
- Imagine that you are looking at a mirror that has a blue frame. Put the problem into the mirror in the form of a word, a phrase or as a symbol that represents the issue. Study it without emotion and get it clear in your mind. Then erase the problem from the mirror and move it to the left.
- Next change the colour of the frame of the mirror to white. Now in your mind's eye, picture an image of the solution on the mirror. Then picture the solution to the problem in the mirror or, better still, picture the results of the solution. Stay focused on that. See yourself now free of the problem.
- The solution to the problem will emerge in your mind.

Counsellor IT!

Within you is an inner voice that is kind and wise. It speaks quietly so it can sometimes be difficult to hear above the noise of everyday life and your critical inner voice. The Counsellor-It technique is about tapping into that inner wisdom.

- Use the Chill-It relaxation technique to get yourself to an alpha brain wave state.
- Using your imagination, picture that you are surrounded by a soft and glowing white light.

- Think of your favourite place in the world. Next, imagine that you are walking into this favourite place. Picture it in great detail.

- Now imagine that a person is walking towards you. This is your Inner Adviser. Ask the person for their name. What is this person like? Make this scene as real as you possibly can in your mind.

- Have a conversation with your Inner Adviser. Treat this as you would an actual conversation in the real world. Ask for help with your challenge. Give your full attention to what he or she says or does. Remember the answers and advice offered. Conclude the conversation and thank your Inner Adviser for their help and wisdom.

DayBreak Thinking

Borderland IT!

This technique is all about what is known as hypnagogic imagery. Surrealist images will appear in your thoughts during the Borderland-It technique. You can find answers to your challenge by relating these images to your problem.

- You are drowsy just before you drift off to sleep and after you first wake up. This is theta wave thinking. It is a very creative state of mind and is the one needed for this technique to work.

- You can also get yourself into this state of mind by totally relaxing your body, quietening your mind and closing your eyes. Do not fall asleep, though.

- Notice the images that come into your mind.

- Ask yourself questions about these images such as:

- What's puzzling about the images?
- What relationship do the images have to the challenge?
- What new insights do these images give me?
- What's out of place in the images?
- What disturbs me about the images?
- What do the images remind me of?
- What are the similarities between the images and my challenge?
- What associations do they trigger?
- What do the images resemble?

NightTime Thinking

Your mind doesn't stop working when you sleep. Unconscious thinking takes place.

There are many examples of scientific discoveries and Eureka Ideas coming to people in their dreams. For example, Friedrich August Kekulé von Stradonitz said that the ring structure of benzene came to him in a dream where a snake was eating its own tail.

When you sleep on an Ideation Task you increase your chances of coming up with the idea you are seeking. Scientists believe that during sleep the brain may restructure problems and, in so doing, can enable a new insight to be arrived at.

Dream IT!

We dream in pictures. Images that occur in dreams are normally symbolic rather than literal. Dreams reveal things you did not know that you knew. Perhaps our earliest type of thinking was symbolic imagery, which is perhaps one reason why we are drawn to poetry.

When you dream, your thoughts combine and rearrange in ways that would never happen while you're awake. Ideas that can solve your problems can occur while you're asleep. The trick is to prime and set your brain up to do that beforehand and to capture the ideas that pop into your dreams.

- The Dream-It technique has to be used following a day when you have actively been working on your challenge.
- Write down the Ideation Task Statement. Repeat it to yourself either out loud or in your head before you go to sleep.
- Do this for a number of evenings in a row, if necessary.
- Try to wake up earlier than you normally would. This will help you to recall your dream. When you wake up, lie quietly for a while.
- When you've remembered your dream or dreams, write it all down in a notebook that you keep beside your bed.
- Free associate on what you dreamed about.
- Ask questions:
  - How was my dream relevant to my challenge?
  - Who was in it?
  - How does this relate?
  - Does it change the nature of my question?
  - What elements can help solve my problem?
  - What associations does it conjure up?

Superconcious Thinking

The ultimate source of all Eureka Ideas and acts of creativity is what is called the Superconscious Mind. The previous steps you have taken in *The MultipleMind Method* will now trigger the activation of it.

The great Austrian psychoanalyst, Carl Jung, came up with the term. He believed that the combined wisdom and knowledge of all the ages is to be found in this Superconscious Mind. This power has also been called infinite intelligence, the universal subconscious mind and the collective unconscious.

Ralph Waldo Emerson called it the oversoul and is quoted as saying: "We live in the lap of an immense intelligence that, when we are in its presence, we realize that it is far beyond our human mind."

Whatever you choose to call it, it is a mind that is above and outside all other minds or intelligences. Its power is available to you right now.

Whenever you come across a great achievement of any kind that strikes a chord, you are a witness to a creation of the Superconscious Mind. It can access any item of information stored in your conscious and subconscious minds along with – and this is the weird part – information and ideas outside of your own experience. It actually is an unseen power which lies outside your own mind.

Think about when you've had ideas that have come to you and you've wondered where they've come from. It is not unusual for two people separated by thousands of miles to come up with the same idea at the same time. So many breakthrough scientific discoveries came about in this way.

When you are on the same wavelength as another person you will often have the same thoughts as them at the same time during the day. Has this ever happened to you? This is an example of your Superconscious Mind at work.

The MultipleMind Method triggers the Superconscious Mind. The actions you need to take and the attitudes you need to adopt to trigger it are part of The MultipleMind Method. For example, the Superconscious Mind works best when the goals are clear, when there is a spirit of faith and when it is imperative that a problem is solved.

The Superconscious Mind needs to know exactly what you are looking for. It needs crystal clear goals that you are completely committed to. It needs to know that you're going to act on its ideas. Otherwise, it says to itself: "What's the point?"

The Superconscious Mind needs to know that you have belief. The more you believe in it and in your ability to achieve your goal, the faster it seems to work.

It also works when you concentrate fully on something or when you're not thinking about it at all. In other words, it comes into play at both ends of the thinking and concentration spectrum. It does not work when you are simply mulling things over. Which is what most of us do for most of the time when it comes to seeking ideas and answers to our problems, isn't it?

When these factors are in place, the Superconscious Mind releases a continuous flow of energy and generates the Eureka Idea and the other resources needed.

Your attitude is crucial when it comes to your Superconscious Mind. It works best when you:

- are thinking clearly;
- are calm and confident; and
- have faith and accept and believe that everything that happens is moving you towards the attainment of your goal.

It's as if your Superconscious Mind comes alive when you adopt this attitude.

Notice how successful people are tremendously clear when it comes to knowing what they want. They also are calm and confident in their ability to achieve success. Successful people think and talk about what they want, and unsuccessful people talk about what they don't want.

Step 6 Illumination

This is it! This is the step in the process when the Eureka Idea you've been working on will strike you. This is when the proverbial light bulb will go off inside your head. Hence why this stage in the process is called Illumination. The insight you've been seeking will finally arrive.

Studies have looked at brain activity at the moment when people have either discovered for themselves or been given the answer to a problem. The data shows that the brain activity mainly occurs in the right hemisphere of the brain. The research also shows that when people have an insight in this way the idea they come up with is normally complete and precise. When people come up with an answer in other ways the idea is normally partial and incomplete.

The Eureka Idea will hit you suddenly and unexpectedly. Rejoice! Have a party and get ready for the next stage where your Eureka Idea is transformed from a concept into reality.

How will you know that your idea is a true Eureka Idea?

You'll know. You'll feel it. Here are the three tell-tale signs.

- The idea will be 100% complete.

- The idea will be a blinding flash of the obvious. It will be so obvious that you'll wonder why you never thought of it before.

- You will feel joy and elation and you will want to get started with the idea right away. You will feel inspired by your idea.

As you know, a Eureka Idea is the result of superconscious thinking. For this reason your Superconscious Mind will now generate a continuous flow of ideas and energy to help you move forward with your Eureka Idea.

The Superconscious Mind has been called a form of 'free energy.' This energy is made available to you any time that you become excited or inspired about achieving something important. With it, you will be able to work for hour after hour without tiring.

Reassure yourself

There is no harm in double checking your idea against your Ideation Task Statement. As a Eureka Idea, it will tick all of the boxes.

Try to be as objective as possible. Divorce yourself from your idea and view it from a cool and detached perspective. Get the opinions of a few outsiders also. Friends or relatives are rarely useful because they usually lack objectivity.

Ask yourself the following questions about the idea.

- Is it effective and efficient? In other words, will it offer the intended results?

- It is the timing right?

- Is it feasible?

- Is it simple?

Step 7
Fruition

> *"Few ideas are in themselves practical. It is for want of imagination in applying them that they fail. The creative process does not end with an idea-it only starts with an idea."* John Arnold

Following through with an idea is as important as having one. You don't want to become that person who is always saying at parties, "I had this great idea once. If only I'd done something with it."

You must have conviction in your ideas. Even if you think it's not perfect yet, get going with it anyway. You can perfect it later.

You have your magical Eureka Idea but you will also have a large number of other new ideas. Go through them. Label them as either:

- simple or complex;
- expensive or inexpensive to implement;
- time-consuming or quick to put into place; or
- crazy and bold or sensible and safe.

Do not discard any ideas. All of the ideas will help you in some way with your future thinking. Some of the ideas might also be shaped into usable ideas. There will be:

- usable ideas which are concrete and can be put into action straightaway;
- unusable ideas that are valuable concepts nonetheless; and
- germ ideas that have potential but need a lot more work.

"I start where the last man left off."
Thomas Edison

There are many ways that you can turn germ ideas into usable ones. For example, if the idea is basically a good one but would be too expensive to create in the way that was originally envisioned, might there be a market for a cheaper version of the same idea?

"Everyone who's ever taken a shower has an idea. It's the person who gets out of the shower, dries off and does something about it who makes the difference." Nolan Bushnell

Now, make it happen

Your idea will come to nothing if you don't take action to make it happen. It's what separates the dreamers from the achievers. So go for it!

The good news is that your Superconscious Mind is now on board because you're working on a Eureka Idea. This means that the ability to automatically and continually solve the problems that will hit you along the way will be with you. Your Superconscious Mind will also give you the lessons and experiences that you need to succeed in the form of setbacks, problems, frustrations and temporary failures.

Be aware that hunches or flashes of inspiration that your Superconscious Mind gives you are time-sensitive. You should act on them there and then.

Here is a powerful 7-step plan that will ensure that your Eureka Idea will come into being.

1. Nourish your desire and your belief that you can do it. Resolve to take an action every day towards making it happen, no matter what. By doing that you will build your belief and strengthen your desire. Start small if need be. Each time you achieve a goal, stretch yourself again. Challenge your comfort zone.

2. You already know the importance of writing things down. Write down what you're trying to achieve in clear, vivid detail. Unless you write it down, it's just a wish. Set deadlines so that you'll know that you're making progress.

3. List all the obstacles you'll have to overcome. You now have a powerful set of problem solving techniques to defeat them when you meet them.

4. List the people you will need to get to know along with the groups and organisations you may need to join.

5. Make a plan. Make it complete in every detail. Set priorities.

6. Visualise what your Eureka Idea will look like when it becomes a reality. Get a clear mental picture and see that picture in your mind often.

7. Along the way you will need determination. Resolve to persist until you achieve. Never, never give up.

"Your persistence is, in fact, the true measure of your belief in yourself and your ability to succeed. Each time that you persist in the face of adversity and disappointment, you build the habit of persistence." Brian Tracy

Congratulations

"Inspiration exists, but it has to find you working." Pablo Picasso

You are now an Ideas Person. You now know how to generate a Eureka Idea any time you want and for any situation you face.

The MultipleMind Method is a powerful tool. The ability to have a Eureka Idea is not a talent that some people are born with and others are not. This is a mental skill that anyone can learn. The *Ideation software* program is inside everyone's brain waiting to be used. The more you practice this, the better you will get at it.

As you've learned, generating Eureka Ideas is hard work. But, my goodness, it's worth it. When great ideas strike, it's a wonderful feeling.

The world needs Ideas People. We're never going to run out of the need for new ideas. For as long as there are problems to solve, you'll be in demand as an Ideas Person. The need for new ideas and innovation never stops.

You've learned a powerful system for thinking. The quiet voice within you now wants you to go for it. It was your quiet voice that persuaded you to buy this book. Listen to your wise but quiet voice. Ignore the noisy voices around you of people who say you can't do it. Jump out of the box. Do not be held down. Your ideas want to be free. They will set you free as well.

There is a desire for greatness within all of us. Deep down we all want to achieve great things. But often we're scared about our ideas. We are fearful that our ideas will be ridiculed. Don't let that be you.

"Our deepest fear is not that we are inadequate. Our deepest fear is that we are powerful beyond measure. It is our light, not our darkness that most frightens us. We ask ourselves, who am I to be brilliant, gorgeous, talented, and fabulous? Actually, who are you not to be? You are a child of God. Your playing small does not serve the world. There is nothing enlightened about shrinking so that other people won't feel insecure around you. We are all meant to shine, as children do. We were born to make manifest the glory of God that is within us. It's not just in some of us; it's in everyone. And as we let our own light shine, we unconsciously give other people permission to do the same. As we are liberated from our own fear, our presence automatically liberates others." Nelson Mandela

APPENDIX 1 – A SYSTEM FOR SOLVING ENGINEERING PROBLEMS

Whilst working as a patent expert in the Soviet Navy in the 1940s, Genrich S. Altshuller asked himself the question:

- Is there an optimal way to solve problems?

An inventor at the tender age of just 14 and trained as a mechanical engineer, he became curious about the process of invention.

Altshuller's belief was that psychological tools and techniques were great but did not fully meet the *problem solving needs of engineers and inventors*. So he made it his job to develop a theory of invention.

Altshuller reviewed over 200,000 patents over the course of the next few years. What interested him was the problem solving process that lead to the invention. If problem solving principles could be identified and codified, he thought, they could be taught to people to make the process of invention more predictable.

He made it his mission to:

- find an innovation system that would be methodical and reliable and which would not be totally dependent on psychological tools;

- come up with a method which would enable problem solvers to access and to also add to the body of inventive knowledge; and

- ensure the theory followed the general approach to problem solving which inventors were already familiar with.

After years of thorough research Altshuller developed the system he had been searching for. TRIZ is the name he gave it. TRIZ is an acronym in Russian for the phrase 'Theory of Inventive Problem Solving'.

What TRIZ does is pull together the problems, contradictions and solutions in these patents into a theory of inventive problem solving.

The research that Altshuller started has continued and now over 2 million patents have been looked at. They have been categorized by level of inventiveness. The patents have also been studied in the search for principles of innovation.

From TRIZ we know that the same problems have been solved with the same solutions across different industries and sciences. We also know that technology has evolved in the same way across industries and sciences.

Altshuller discovered that over 90% of the problems engineers faced had been solved somewhere before, either in the same or another industry. The same problems had been solved many times over using one of only 40 fundamental inventive principles.

Altshuller categorized the solutions that were patented into five levels.

- Level 1 – just under a third of the solutions were routine design problems solved by methods well known within the specialty.

- Level 2 – 45% of the solutions were minor improvements to an existing system using methods known within the same industry.

- Level 3 – 18% of the solutions were a fundamental improvement to an existing system by methods known outside the particular industry.

- Level 4 – 4% were a new generation that uses a new principle to perform the primary functions of the system.

- Level 5 – 1% of the solutions were a rare scientific discovery or pioneering invention of essentially a new system.

TRIZ is a 4-step process.

Stage 1 is *Identify the Problem*

- This involves identifying:

    - the system that needs solving;

    - its operating environment;

    - its resource requirements;

    - its primary useful function;

    - its harmful effects; and

    - the ideal result.

Stage 2 is *Formulate the Problem*

- This is about restating the problem in terms of what the TRIZ methodology refers to as the 'physical contradictions'.

- Altshuller believed that problems stem from contradictions (or trade-offs) between two or more elements. That is, could improving one technical characteristic to solve a problem actually cause other technical characteristics to worsen, resulting in secondary problems arising?

- This step entails asking if there are technical conflicts that might force a trade-off.

Stage 3 is *Search for a Previously Well-Solved Problem*

- Altshuller identified 39 standard technical characteristics that cause conflict. These are called the 39 Engineering Parameters.

- So the idea is to find the contradicting engineering principles –

that is, the principle that needs to be changed and the principle that is an undesirable secondary effect.

Stage 4 is *Look for Analogous Solutions and Adapt to my Solution*

- The next step is to use the 40 inventive principles that Altshuller identified as hints to find a solution to the problem.

Let's look at a few of these 40 inventive principles.

- *Segmentation* means to separate into smaller parts.

- *Nesting* means putting one thing inside another like a Russian doll, or fitting things together in some way.

- *Combination* is to bring together things which happen at the same time or in the same place.

- *Spheroidality* involves considering all forms of curves instead of flat surfaces.

- *Inversion* which means doing the opposite of what might seem normal.

Notice how some of these principles are similar to the psychological Colourful Thinking techniques used in *The MultipleMind Method*. The principle behind *Inversion* is similar to the *Overturn-It* technique.

TRIZ was used to fix the problem of invisible fractures when using artificial diamonds for tool making. Conventional diamond cutting methods often resulted in new fractures which did not show up until the diamond was in use.

What was needed was a way to split the diamond crystals along their natural fractures without causing added damage. A method from another industry – food canning – was identified as analogous and was successfully adapted.

The process for splitting green peppers and removing the seeds involves placing the green peppers in a hermetic chamber where the air pressure is increased to 8 atmospheres. The peppers shrink and fracture at the stem. Then the pressure is rapidly dropped causing the peppers to burst at the weakest point and the seed pod to be ejected.

A similar technique was successfully applied to diamond cutting. It means that the crystals now split along their natural fracture lines with no additional damage.

TRIZ has developed over the years to the point where large and small companies are using it to solve everyday problems and to develop strategies for the future of technology. It is used at companies such as Ford, Procter and Gamble and Motorola.

The 40 Inventive Principles

1. Segmentation
   - Split an object into independent parts.

   - Make an object sectional.

   - Increase the degree of an object's segmentation.

2. Extraction
   - Remove or separate a disturbing part or property from an object or remove or separate only the necessary part or property.

3. Local Quality
   - Transition from a homogeneous structure of an object or outside environment/action to a heterogeneous structure.

   - Have different parts of the object carry out different functions.

- Place each part of the object under conditions most favourable for its operation.

4. Asymmetry

- Replace a symmetrical form with an asymmetrical form.

- If an object is already asymmetrical, increase the degree of asymmetry.

5. Combining

- Combine in space homogeneous objects or objects destined for contiguous operations.

- Combine in time homogeneous or contiguous operations.

6. Universality

- Have the object perform multiple functions, thereby eliminating the need for some other object(s).

7. Nesting

- Contain the object inside another which, in turn, is placed inside a third object.

- Pass an object through a cavity of another object.

8. Counterweight

- Compensate for the object's weight by joining with another object that has a lifting force.

- Compensate for the weight of an object by interaction with an environment providing aerodynamic or hydrodynamic forces.

9. Prior counter-action

- Perform a counter-action in advance.

- If the object is (or will be) under tension, provide anti-tension in advance.

10. Prior action

- Carry out all or part of the required action in advance.

- Arrange objects so they can go into action in a timely matter and from a convenient position.

11. Cushion in advance

- Compensate for the relatively low reliability of an object by countermeasures taken in advance.

12. Equipotentiality

- Change the working conditions so that an object need not be raised or lowered.

13. Inversion

- Instead of an action dictated by the specifications of the problem, implement an opposite action.

- Make a moving part of the object or the outside environment immovable and the non-moving part movable.

- Turn the object upside-down.

14. Spheroidality

- Replace linear parts or flat surfaces with curved ones; replace cubical shapes with spherical shapes.

- Use rollers, balls or spirals.

- Replace a linear motion with rotating movement; utilize a centrifugal force.

15. Dynamicity

- Make an object or its environment automatically adjust for optimal performance at each stage of operation.

- Divide an object into elements which can change position relative to each other.

- If an object is immovable, make it movable or interchangeable.

16. Partial or overdone action
   - If it is difficult to obtain 100% of a desired effect, achieve somewhat more or less to greatly simplify the problem.

17. Moving to a new dimension
   - Remove problems with moving an object in a line by two-dimensional movement – that is, along a plane.
   - Use a multi-layered assembly of objects instead of a single layer.
   - Incline the object or turn it on its side.

18. Mechanical vibration
   - Set an object into oscillation.
   - If oscillation exists, increase its frequency, even as far as ultrasonic.
   - Use the resonant frequency.
   - Instead of mechanical vibrations, use piezovibrators.
   - Use ultrasonic vibrations in conjunction with an electromagnetic field.

19. Periodic action
   - Replace a continuous action with a periodic (pulsed) one.
   - If an action is already periodic, change its frequency.
   - Use pulsed between impulses to provide additional action.

20. Continuity of a useful action
   - Carry out an action continuously (that is, without pauses), where all parts of an object operate at full capacity.

- Remove idle and intermediate motions.

21. Rushing through
- Perform harmful or hazardous operations at very high speed.

22. Convert harm into benefit
- Utilize harmful factors or environmental effects to obtain a positive effect.

- Remove a harmful factor by combining it with another harmful factor.

- Increase the amount of harmful action until it ceases to be harmful.

23. Feedback
- Introduce feedback.

- If feedback already exists, reverse it.

24. Mediator
- Use an intermediary object to transfer or carry out an action.

- Temporarily connect an object to another one that is easy to remove.

25. Self-service
- Make the object service itself and carry out supplementary and repair operations.

- Make use of wasted material and energy.

26. Copying
- Use a simple and inexpensive copy instead of an object which is complex, expensive, fragile or inconvenient to operate.

- Replace an object by its optical copy or image. A scale can be used to reduce or enlarge the image.

- If visible optical copies are used, replace them with infrared or ultraviolet copies.

27. Inexpensive, short-lived object for expensive, durable one
- Replace an expensive object by a collection of inexpensive ones, forgoing properties (e.g. longevity).

28. Replacement of a mechanical system
- Replace a mechanical system by an optical, acoustical or olfactory (odour) system.

- Use an electrical, magnetic or electromagnetic field for interaction with the object.

- Replace fields, for example:
  - stationary fields with moving fields;
  - fixed fields with those which change in time; or
  - random fields with structured fields.

- Use a field in conjunction with ferromagnetic particles.

29. Pneumatic or hydraulic construction
- Replace solid parts of an object by gas or liquid. These parts can use air or water for inflation, or use air or hydrostatic cushions.

30. Flexible membranes or thin film
- Replace traditional constructions with those made from flexible membranes or thin film.

- Isolate an object from its environment using flexible membranes or thin film.

31. Use of porous material
- Make an object porous or add porous elements (inserts, covers, etc.).
- If an object is already porous, fill the pores in advance with some substance.

32. Changing the colour
- Change the colour of an object or its surroundings.
- Change the degree of translucency of an object or processes which are difficult to see.
- Use coloured additives to observe objects or processes which are difficult to see.
- If such additives are already used, employ luminescent traces or tracer elements.

33. Homogeneity
- Make those objects which interact with a primary object out of the same material or material that is close to it in behaviour.

34. Rejecting and regenerating parts
- After it has completed its function or become useless, reject or modify (e.g. discard, dissolve, evaporate) an element of an object.
- Immediately restore any part of an object which is exhausted or depleted.

35. Transformation of the physical and chemical states of an object
- Change an object's aggregate state, density distribution, degree of flexibility, temperature.

36. Phase transformation

- Implement an effect developed during the phase transition of a substance. For instance, during the change of volume, liberation or absorption of heat.

37. Thermal expansion

- Use a material which expands or contracts with heat.

- Use various materials with different coefficients of heat expansion.

38. Use strong oxidizers

- Replace normal air with enriched air.

- Replace enriched air with oxygen.

- Treat an object in air or in oxygen with ionizing radiation.

- Use ionized oxygen.

39. Inert environment

- Replace the normal environment with an inert one.

- Carry out the process in a vacuum.

40. Composite materials

- Replace a homogeneous material with a composite one.

The 39 Engineering Parameters

1   Weight of moving object

2   Weight of stationary object

3   Length of moving object

4   Length of stationary object

5   Area of moving object

6   Area of stationary object

7   Volume of moving object

8   Volume of stationary object

9   Speed

10   Force (Intensity)

11   Stress or pressure

12   Shape

13   Stability of the object's composition

14   Strength

15   Duration of action of moving object

16   Duration of action by stationary object

17   Temperature

18   Illumination intensity

19   Use of energy by moving object

20   Use of energy by stationary object

21   Power

22   Loss of Energy

23   Loss of substance

24   Loss of Information

25   Loss of Time

26   Quantity of substance/the matter

27   Reliability

28   Measurement accuracy

Resources

www.wizeeka.com

- Idea Generation Sessions
- Inspirational Corporate Away Days
- Collaboration Training

Brain Performance Consultant

www.steveroche.com

 **@stevewroche**